RAND NATIONAL DEFENSE RESEARCH INSTITUTE

Sea Power and American Interests in the Western Pacific

David C. Gompert

The research described in this report was conducted within the International Security and Defense Policy Center of the RAND National Defense Research Institute, a federally funded research and development center sponsored by the Office of the Secretary of Defense, the Joint Staff, the Unified Combatant Commands, the Navy, the Marine Corps, the defense agencies, and the defense Intelligence Community.

Library of Congress Cataloging-in-Publication Data

Gompert, David C.
Sea power and American interests in the western Pacific / David C. Gompert ; foreword by James Dobbins.
pages cm
Includes bibliographical references.
ISBN 978-0-8330-7890-2 (pbk. : alk. paper)
1. Sea power—Pacific Area. 2. Sea power—China. 3. Sea power—United States. 4. China—Strategic aspects. 5. United States—Relations—China. 6. China—Relations—United States. 7. Geopolitics—China. 8. Naval strategy. I. Title.

V25.G65 2012
359'.030916—dc23 2013010138

Cover photo: USS Connecticut *(BB-18) running speed trials off the Maine coast, 1906. Photographed by Enrique Muller. U.S. Naval Historical Foundation photograph.*

Published 2013 by the RAND Corporation
1776 Main Street, P.O. Box 2138, Santa Monica, CA 90407-2138
1200 South Hayes Street, Arlington, VA 22202-5050
4570 Fifth Avenue, Suite 600, Pittsburgh, PA 15213-2665
RAND URL: http://www.rand.org/
To order RAND documents or to obtain additional information, contact
Distribution Services: Telephone: (310) 451-7002;
Fax: (310) 451-6915; Email: order@rand.org

Foreword

by James Dobbins

Referring to how "those far distant, storm-beaten ships, upon which the Grand Army never looked, stood between it and the dominion of the world," Captain Alfred Thayer Mahan both described Britain's successful blockade of Napoleonic France and sought thereby to persuade Americans that their own nation's manifest destiny should not stop at the water's edge. Mahan's massively popular *The Influence of Sea Power upon History* was signally successful in so doing, becoming part of the intellectual backdrop to America's acquisition of Caribbean and Far Eastern colonies and the construction of a world-class battle fleet.

Unfortunately, Mahan's thesis also impressed many influential Germans and Japanese. Their aspirations were dashed at Jutland and Midway. The last of these battles gave the United States unchallenged mastery of the world's oceans, a position it continues to occupy 70 years later.

Today, China is emerging as a potential competitor. In this volume, David Gompert asks what these earlier contests can tell us about that which is now on the horizon. History teaches many lessons. The difficulty is picking the right one. Well aware of this, David offers herein reflections on three encounters between rising and declining sea powers. Two of these ended in war, that between Germany and the United Kingdom in 1914 and between Japan and the United States in 1941. The third, that between the United Kingdom and the United States, led to a gradual and largely amicable transfer of first regional and then global predominance from one navy to the other.

None of these outcomes is particularly appealing, as David Gompert's analysis makes clear. Must America ultimately fight for or cede its naval primacy? If one projects recent Chinese and American economic growth rates several decades into the future, it becomes hard to envisage how one outcome or the other can be avoided. How long would an otherwise preeminent China be content to see a smaller, poorer, less powerful rival dominate the world's sea-lanes? How long would an otherwise weaker America wish to guard global trade routes for China's trade at America's expense? These are the questions with which this important study grapples.

Of course, China may not continue growing faster than America. After all, Japan did not. Even if China does, will it inevitably choose to challenge America's maritime superiority?

Maritime competition between the United States and China is already being shaped by new cyber, space, and other technologies of which Admirals Nelson, von Tirpitz, and Yamamoto never dreamed. The geo-political and geo-economic environment in which this competition is waged has also evolved. Never in human history have the benefits of peace, in terms of rapidly improving material well-being, been so great, nor the consequences of war, in terms of nuclear devastation, been so catastrophic. As a result, interstate conflict has become exceedingly rare. Indeed, no two major powers have gone to war with each other in more than half a century. Great nations still compete for power, influence, and wealth, but do so upon a somewhat different set of assumptions about the risks of conflict and the rewards of cooperation.

For these reasons, it would be imprudent to assume that Sino-American naval rivalry must end like any of those cited in this volume. It would be equally imprudent, however, to assume otherwise, as this study makes clear. The past may not chart the future, but it's the only map we have. Maritime competition with China will almost certainly increase over the coming years. At the very least, China will challenge American dominance of the seas immediately adjacent to it. David Gompert illuminates herein the prospects for that contest in the light of current and future capabilities, existing American and Chinese strategies, and the prior experience of such great-power rivalries.

Preface

The idea for this book originated during research done by the author and Phil Saunders of the National Defense University on the mutual strategic vulnerabilities of China and the United States. That work, which culminated in *The Paradox of Power: Sino-American Strategic Restraint in an Era of Vulnerability* (National Defense University Press, 2012), proposed measures the two powers could take to reduce the dangers of conflict in the nuclear, anti-satellite, and cyber-war domains. But it left dangling one problem, arguably as important: the maritime domain—in particular, the looming competition and potential confrontation between Chinese and American sea power in the Western Pacific and adjacent seas.

Just as that region has entered a period of change, owing to China's expanding power, so is the nature of sea power changing. As a consequence, great uncertainty surrounds the question of who will control these vital waters—a question of importance for the United States, China, the rest of the region, and the world. With global economic integration, reliance on sea-borne trade and sea-based resources is growing. So is interest in cooperative maritime security, an idea advanced by the world's leading naval power, the United States. At the same time, technology is increasing the vulnerability of naval vessels and shipping on the oceans' surface. If the latter development means that the maritime domain may become less secure, the former development suggests an alternative to maritime competition and confrontation. Indeed, the rush of technology could push rivals at sea to become partners at sea instead.

With regard to both developments, the future relationship between American and Chinese sea power—in classical terms, the "established power" and the "rising power"—is central, especially in East Asian waters. This study explores that relationship along several dimensions: theoretical, historical, economic, geo-political, and technological. It does so from the standpoint of U.S. interests, though with an eye on Chinese and other foreign interests. The imperative of maritime security and the challenge of vulnerability are not unique to the United States or to the Western Pacific. However, it is on U.S. interests in the Western Pacific that changes in sea power may have their first big effects.

This study comes at a time of heightened recognition of the importance of this region to the world and to the United States. Its findings should be of interest to policymakers, opinion makers, practitioners, and scholars involved in any aspect of Sino-American relations, Asian affairs, naval and maritime questions, or political-military issues in general. While the issues are complex, the author has tried to present them in an accessible way.

This research was conducted within the International Security and Defense Policy Center of the RAND National Defense Research Institute, a federally funded research and development center sponsored by the Office of the Secretary of Defense, the Joint Staff, the Unified Combatant Commands, the Navy, the Marine Corps, the defense agencies, and the defense Intelligence Community.

For more information on the International Security and Defense Policy Center, see http://www.rand.org/nsrd/ndri/centers/isdp.html or contact the director (contact information is provided on the web page).

Contents

Figure and Tables

Figure

Tables

Summary

American power in the Western Pacific has been, is, and will remain largely defined by sea power. Yet China views nearby U.S. sea power as a menacing presence, a counterweight to its regional interests, and a potential barrier to its access to the world's oceans, resources, and markets. It is therefore deploying anti-ship missiles, submarines, and other capabilities that threaten the U.S. surface fleet. China is also expanding its own naval forces in East Asian waters to back its territorial claims, secure its trade approaches, and extend its influence. Because this vital region could become unstable or fall under China's sway if U.S. sea power recedes or is allowed to become vulnerable, the United States can be expected to react to this challenge. Thus, a classic case of an established sea power resisting a rising one is shaping up in the Western Pacific.

Such rivalries have a way of ending up in confrontation and war. Alfred Thayer Mahan (1840–1914), widely recognized as the father of sea-power theory, held that a world power needs overseas access to raw materials and markets to expand its production beyond its consumption and thus grow stronger. Observing how Great Britain's "outsized" Royal Navy enabled its industrial, commercial, and imperial success, he concluded that sea power is key to world power. In turn, sea power demands national—not just naval—consciousness, consensus, commitment, and stamina. As Mahan saw it, rivalry between sea powers is inherent in Darwinian world power-politics. Any sea power worth its salt must be able both to safeguard its maritime access (sea control) and, if need be, to disrupt the access of its rivals (sea denial). The core of sea power, Mahan argued, is the offensive strength of the concentrated battle fleet.

Mahan's ideas shaped the great sea-power rivalries of the late 19th and early 20th centuries. His *The Influence of Sea Power upon History* was compulsory reading for German and Japanese officers, and proponents of American imperialism, notably Theodore Roosevelt, Henry Cabot Lodge, and William Randolph Hearst, appropriated his theories to make their case. Having established continental control and developed an industrial economy, the United States turned to sea power in order to obtain possessions, achieve world power, and rid its hemisphere of foreign presence.

Great Britain, the dominant sea power of the time, chose not to oppose U.S. sea power because it faced more severe dangers elsewhere and competing demands for resources and social reform at home. Imperial Germany directly challenged British sea supremacy, which was seen as a threat to its overseas access and an impediment to becoming a world power. London regarded the combination of Germany's hegemonic potential in Europe and its challenge to British sea power as a strategic threat and responded by further strengthening the Royal Navy and aligning with its old enemy and Europe's weaker power, France. Anglo-German animosity, stoked by the race to build dreadnoughts, contributed to conditions that led to World War I.

Although sea power did not decide that war's outcome, the pattern Mahan posited of rising powers challenging established ones resumed, now in the Pacific. Japan's sinking of the Russian fleet in the Strait of Tsushima in 1905 had already signaled its arrival as a great, if regional, sea power. With Britain fatigued and America isolationist in the 1920s, Japan sought control of East Asian waters to acquire possessions, markets, and resources needed to sustain its own industrialization. Japan relentlessly expanded its navy, built a formidable force of aircraft carriers, and honed the skills of its skippers and sailors. Belatedly, the United States responded by increasing and deploying its fleet forward in the 1930s, threatening the lifelines on which Japan depended to pursue conquests and expand its war-making capacity. Japan felt compelled to attack Pearl Harbor. America's industrial might and superior aircraft carriers prevailed, annihilating Japan's sea power and, ironically, making it dependent thereafter on that of its victor.

Of these three cases, the most encouraging, obviously, is the Anglo-American one, which ended not in war but in maritime coexistence, cooperation, and eventual alliance. However, the United States is not about to defer to China in East Asia as Britain deferred to America in the Western Hemisphere. At the other extreme, the violent climax of Japanese-American sea-power rivalry does not ordain a similar result for China and the United States; after all, China is not engaged in aggression and the United States has not threatened to sever its sea links, as in the Japanese-American case.

The Anglo-German case, which also ended badly, seems more analogous to the Sino-American case. This raises the question of how Britain and Germany might have resolved their rivalry peacefully and even cooperatively. In fact, British and German statesmen lacked the vision and political clout to resist the drive of their naval strategists, build on common interests in maritime security, and thus avert a costly arms race and, perhaps, war. More fundamentally, neither Britain's strategy of wielding the threat to deny sea access to any adversary nor Germany's determination to negate that British threat permitted compromise. For China and the United States today, the Anglo-German dreadnought race is a cautionary tale.

Today, while the United States and China have convergent global interests, they are at loggerheads in East Asia, from Korea to Taiwan to Southeast Asia. Given the importance of U.S. sea power to regional security and American influence, conditions seem set for the sort of rivalry that ended in violence in the Anglo-German and U.S.-Japanese cases. China's vast claims in the resource-rich South China and East China Seas are causing U.S. allies and others to look to the United States for backing. Despite common Chinese and U.S. interests in maritime security—95 percent of China's trade and 90 percent of U.S. trade is sea-borne—a clash between the rising and established sea powers is brewing in East Asian waters.

While the Chinese have not embraced global sea power, in Mahan's sense of the term, they are moving from coastal defense to extending their naval reach into disputed water to protection of trade routes. They are also collaborating with U.S. and other navies to combat piracy off Africa's east coast; but such modest endeavors, far from the Western Pacific, in no way imply Chinese acceptance of U.S. naval strike forces near China. Of greatest concern, the Chinese are exploiting information technology—for sensing, networking, and guiding platforms and weapons—to improve and extend their targeting of surface ships with missiles, submarines, and cyber weapons. (In contrast, Chinese aircraft carriers will present a negligible threat to the U.S. fleet and be quite vulnerable.) While the Chinese are presently concentrating on such anti-naval—essentially sea-denial—capabilities, these constitute sea power no less than traditional surface naval forces do. Sea power, after all, is not power *upon* the sea but power *of* the sea—a distinction Mahan did not make in his world of battleships and gunnery.

Defending surface fleets against extended-range missiles and quiet submarines is difficult, expensive, and of diminishing utility in the face of China's accelerating anti-naval build-up. With technologies at hand, neither ballistic missile defense nor anti-submarine warfare can keep up with the offensive enhancements of a large, capable, and resolute rival. Because of their strike capabilities and importance in U.S. military intervention in East Asia, U.S. aircraft carriers are in the crosshairs of Chinese strategy and Chinese weapons. Both Mahan's 19th-century dictum that the key to sea power is concentrated naval force and the 20th century's application of that dictum—the carrier—are being overtaken by 21st-century targeting and networking technology. As the battleship became vulnerable to and marginalized by the aircraft carrier by World War II, missiles and submarines will endanger the aircraft carrier and its primacy in the Western Pacific in the years to come.

The U.S. Navy, in cooperation with the U.S. Air Force, is responding to this adverse trend with preparations to counter China's anti-naval and other anti-access capabilities, under the heading "Air-Sea Battle." While this is an option worth having, using it would be escalatory, in that most targets are on Chinese territory. It could also be destabilizing, given that it would be most effective if employed at the very outset of a conflict, thus increasing China's incentive to strike first and early, or even preemptively. Moreover, because Air-Sea Battle relies on computer networks for command, control, and targeting, it is exposed to Chinese cyber-attacks. It is a potentially risky military strategy on which the United States ought not to depend, and it will not solve the vulnerability problem.

If there is a technological remedy, it lies in outflanking Chinese targeting, figuratively speaking. Taking full advantage of networking, the United States can and should shift toward more distributed, numerous, diverse, elusive, small, long-range, and hard-to-find naval strike forces, while also exploiting two promising offensive technologies: drones and cyber-war. A more survivable U.S. strike posture along these lines would be neither escalatory nor destabilizing. Rather, by facing China with a far more complex targeting challenge, it would discourage Chinese preemptive attack, obviate the need for U.S. preemptive attack, and allow time for a crisis to be defused. Carriers will remain invaluable for the United States in other regions and will surely remain in its global fleet; but their vulnerability is becoming an operational liability in the Western Pacific. As this reality becomes apparent, the carrier's potency in East Asian politics will also recede. Conversely, more survivable, if less conspicuous, U.S. sea power would sustain U.S. influence and interests in the region.

Eventually, even more distributed and less visible U.S. forces may be targetable, especially with the advent of cyber-war. By that time, U.S. sea power and thus U.S. influence and war-fighting ability in the Western Pacific may be eclipsed by Chinese anti-naval and naval forces. In any case, the United States is unlikely to shift rapidly to more survivable sea power, given the long lead-times required, fiscal constraints, and institutional-industrial inertia.

Given technological trends, an unfavorable time-line, and the fact that the United States cannot retreat from the waters of this vital region, it should also pursue a political alternative to head-to-head sea-power rivalry—one that engages its regional partners and, ideally, China itself. With the rapid expansion of sea-borne commerce and sea-based resource extraction that has accompanied globalization, the idea of collective maritime security, first championed by Admiral Mike Mullen (in 2005, when he was Chief of Naval Operations), has gained momentum in a number of regions other than East Asia. If the targeting and networking revolutions invalidate Mahan's prescription for concentrated naval power, U.S. leadership in organizing cooperative maritime security in East Asia may invalidate his premise that sea power is necessarily adversarial. Even as the dominant sea power, the United States cannot provide sea control in every ocean, littoral, and choke-point where it is needed in today's world. Just as the United States is capitalizing on its strength at sea to mobilize and lead others toward cooperative maritime security elsewhere, it should try to do so in the Western Pacific, where the stakes are greatest.

More specifically, the United States should propose and pursue an East Asian maritime partnership, inviting to join all states that share its interest in assured access and passage. Such cooperation could be predicated on the norms that disputes should be settled nonviolently and that civilian shipping engaged in peaceful, peacetime trade should not be threatened. These norms could be buttressed by enhanced maritime information-sharing, crisis consultations, joint exercises and operations (e.g., against non-state threats), and measures to avoid incidents. Realistically, resolving the region's complex maritime legal disputes should not be a precondition for creating or joining the partnership; but a pledge to refrain from force in the meantime should be. Neither the United States nor China would be expected to reduce its sea-power capabilities or relinquish any of its options in the event of war. While such undertakings would not preclude naval/anti-naval competition or conflict outright, they could reduce mistrust and mistakes of the sort that are more likely than rational forethought to trigger Sino-U.S. hostilities.

The goal of East Asian maritime cooperation would not be to exclude China but instead to convince it to join. The participation of the region's increasingly capable navies would encourage China to join and bolster a multilateral approach to security or else to oppose and divorce itself from a formidable naval grouping. Apart from China, a number of East Asian states are developing some of the world's most advanced naval and anti-naval forces; while the United States and China's oceanic neighbors should not seek to align against China, China should take care not to give them cause to do so by rejecting a cooperative arrangement. Indications that some Chinese are getting worried about regional isolation—owing to China's growing power and assertiveness—could enable its political leaders to overrule the almost certain opposition of its military.

Thus, the United States can at least open the door to the sort of maritime cooperation that eluded British and German statesmen before rivalry at sea became too intense to halt. It might well be that Chinese nationalism, weak civilian control of the military, and suspicion of American motives would make China's accession unlikely, at least for now. Chinese ambivalence toward Sino-American military-to-military contacts over the years suggests a need for American patience and persistence. A cooperative approach to maritime security in East Asia may be a long shot and might get watered down (forgive the pun). But the advantages of an arrangement that could build familiarity and confidence while reducing dangers at sea are substantial. Moreover, as noted, the United States would not limit its capabilities or its freedom of action in the event of war. It is a high-return, low-risk idea worth trying. In parallel, technology permits the United States to transform its sea-power posture in the Western Pacific to one more survivable, operationally and politically, whether maritime cooperation ensues or not.

In sum, the United States should move beyond dependence on concentrated surface forces while also pursuing a cooperative alternative to history's classic reaction to a rising sea power. China and the United States have powerful reasons to avoid confrontation and the risk of war in East Asia. Because growing capabilities for sea denial may deprive both of assured sea control, the pursuit of strategic advantage at sea may leave both with diminished security at sea. The United States has technological and political options that, in tandem, can add crisis stability, lessen the intensity of sea-power rivalry, and reduce the danger of conflict, even as it shifts toward a posture that would enable it to prevail were conflict with China to occur.

Acknowledgments

The author thanks several people for their inspiration and help in the thinking and effort that went into this book. L. Paul Bremer, a colleague and friend of many decades, was the first to pose what turned out to be two pivotal questions: How might the British have averted naval rivalry and then confrontation with Imperial Germany in the years prior to World War I? What can we learn from their failure to do so that could shed light on how the United States ought to deal with China? In reading and discussing drafts of this book, Ambassador Bremer provided incisive and constructive criticism.

Likewise, James Dobbins, another "old" associate and friend, was a source of penetrating questions and original ideas regarding all three of the historical cases, as well as the Sino-American case at hand. As it turns out, Ambassador Dobbins is as good at history as he is at diplomacy and policymaking. His support in lining up the resources that enabled this work to be done is much appreciated, as is his willingness to write the book's Foreword—a fine essay in its own right.

A goodly share of the understanding of Chinese thinking and strategy that informs this book is the result of the author's collaboration with Phillip Saunders of the National Defense University. While he may not agree with all of the analysis and findings here, Dr. Saunders will see that the influence of his writings and our conversations is significant.

Nothing beats getting tough reviews from well-qualified peers to push an author to improve his analysis and writing. I was fortunate that David Shlapak of RAND and Lawrence Cavaiola of the United States Naval Academy were meticulous and thoughtful in their reactions to earlier versions of this work. Both questioned important assumptions and conclusions. If the final product is thought to be good, they deserve a lot of the credit.

For their able research assistance, I also want to thank Samuel Berkowitz and Celene von Dutzman, both of whom provided significant input and a keen eye for accuracy and clarity.

If, despite all such help, this book contains any errors of detail or logic, they are the author's alone.

Abbreviations

A2	anti-access
A2AD	anti-access, area-denial
AD	area-denial
ASAT	anti-satellite
ASW	anti-submarine warfare
BMD	ballistic missile defense
C4ISR	command, control, communications, computers, intelligence, surveillance, and reconnaissance
GDP	gross domestic product
PACOM	U.S. Pacific Command
PLA	People's Liberation Army
PLAN	PLA Navy
WMD	weapons of mass destruction

CHAPTER ONE

Introduction

"Command of the sea is not 'naval.' It is one of national policy, national security, and national obligation." —A. T. Mahan[1]

Sea Power and the Western Pacific: Importance, Scope, and Definition

Since Commodore Matthew Perry arrived, uninvited, with a squadron of U.S. warships in Edo (now Tokyo) Bay in 1854, American Pacific power has been defined by American sea power.[2] It was sea power that enabled the United States to assert itself in these waters and lands around them in the late 1800s. During the 20th century, U.S. fleets patrolled and, when called upon, controlled the Western Pacific, confirming that the United States has a Pacific calling to go with its Atlantic heritage. Today, with its heavy reliance on East Asian products and markets, the economic interests of the United States in the region are greater than ever. The Asia-Pacific share of total U.S. trade has risen from 5 percent in 1900 to 15 percent in 1950 to 30 percent today, larger even than U.S. trade with the rest of North America.[3]

Meanwhile, China's rise as a great power presents the United States with both the risk of regional strife and the chance for global cooperation. As the United States recovers from its decade-long preoccupation with extremist threats in the Middle East and South Asia and

[1] Alfred T. Mahan, "The Importance of Command of the Sea: For an Adequate Navy, and More," *Scientific American*, Vol. 105, No. 24, December 1911, p. 512.

[2] Japan's leaders acquiesced in Perry's visit because they thought the country was defenseless.

[3] U.S. Census Bureau, *2012 Statistical Abstract*, Washington, D.C., 2012.

turns its attention to East Asia, it is again sea power, though in forms yet unsettled, that will lend strength to the United States' diplomacy and its ability to wage war if need be. At this juncture, it is important to assess the implications of China's growing power, depending on how it is used, for America's renewed interests, depending on how they are defined. Although the sea is only one of the domains in which Chinese power affects U.S. interests, it is as crucial as any, and the subject of this book.

At times, including ours, the United States has sought and gained predominant sea power, hence *sea control*—defined by two prominent 20th-century proponents of sea power as "the ability to use the sea in defiance of rivals."[4] In a vast region of capable nation-states and economic vitality, where sea-borne trade is crucial, a policy of sea control can invite challenge: After all, one state's sea control can be seen by others as a threat to their own access, i.e., *sea denial.*

Because these time-weathered terms are still useful, if sometimes misunderstood, it is worth clarifying them up front. In essence, sea control is defensive, and sea denial is offensive. The former is the ability to assure continuous freedom to navigate in any and all important waters of choice. The latter is the ability or action *at least temporarily* to deny others access to waters considered important.[5] Because the ultimate purpose of oceanic access is trade, sea control, strictly speaking, is meant to protect shipping, and sea denial is meant to menace it. For our purposes, control includes being able safely to operate one's navy where one wishes, and denial includes being able to endanger and disrupt such naval operations.

Sea control is not the mirror image of sea denial. It is theoretically possible, if practically unlikely, to have sea control without being able to exercise sea denial—to *enjoy* yet not be able to *prevent* access.

---

[4] E. B. Potter and Chester W. Nimitz, *Sea Power: A Naval History*, Upper Saddle River, N.J.: Prentice-Hall, 1960.

[5] Thanks to Michael McDevitt for an explanation of this important distinction, in "The PLA Navy's Antiaccess Role in a Taiwan Contingency," in Phillip Saunders, Christopher Yung, Michael Swaine, and Andrew Nien-Dzu Yang, eds., *The Chinese Navy: Expanding Capabilities, Evolving Roles*, Washington, D.C.: National Defense University Press, 2011, pp. 191–214.

Conversely, sea denial does not require sea control, since even without assured access there are ways—land-based missiles, for instance—to disrupt an adversary's access.[6] In view of technological trends and Western Pacific geography, we will see that this distinction is of consequence, and that technology is affecting sea control and sea denial differently.

At the same time, there is an obvious correlation between sea control and sea denial, in that the naval capabilities with which a power assures its own access can also be used to deny access to others. The submarine or aircraft carrier that secures a patch of ocean for one's own use can also threaten its use by others. From the Chinese perspective, there is a strong relationship between U.S. sea control and U.S. sea denial in the Western Pacific today, as there was from the Japanese perspective prior to World War II. Imperial Japan viewed American sea power as such a threat to its access to vital raw materials that it felt compelled to go to war. Because the Japanese, correctly, interpreted U.S. strategy as aimed at sea control *and* sea denial, they attacked the main instrument of *both* at Pearl Harbor. In the war thus begun, superior American industrial might and naval prowess brought about the destruction of Japanese aircraft carriers in high-seas battles of unprecedented scale and fury.[7] Ironically, the elimination of Japan's sea power left it dependent on the very American sea power it tried and failed to eliminate.

China, the United States, and the Dynamic of Sea Power

How China interprets and counters U.S. sea power and whether and how the United States can and should try to maintain both sea con-

[6] As an historical example, the Soviet Union could not have achieved sea control but, largely through the use of land-based air power, had modest success in constricting the U.S. Navy's access to waters within striking distance of its territory.

[7] Of course, it was not U.S. naval power alone but its combination with unstoppable island-hopping land-force power and strategic-bombing that brought down Japan's war-fighting and war-making capabilities. Historians still argue about whether U.S. nuclear weapons were essential to cause Japan to surrender.

trol and sea denial in the Western Pacific are questions this book will attempt to answer. At the same time, technological change is complicating these questions: In the late 19th century, the best weapon against the battleship was another battleship; in the middle of the 20th century, the surest way to sink an aircraft carrier was with planes from another aircraft carrier. As the result of major and continuing increases in the range and fidelity of sensors, communications, and weapons, these simple equations have fractured. The capabilities a sea power uses to assure its access are not necessarily the only or even best ones to deny another power's access. It no longer takes a carrier to sink a carrier.

The U.S. Navy is as indispensable as ever to the ability of the United States to conduct its business, secure its interests, fulfill its responsibilities, and maintain stability in this region (and other regions) of critical importance to the American and global economies. Although China and the United States are not inevitable enemies, especially as long as they are economic partners, the expansion of Chinese power is prompting many Asian nations to look to American resolve and muscle for reassurance. Questions have arisen about whether China will become both able and determined to challenge American sea power: able because of its stunning economic and technological development; determined because it sees the U.S. Navy as threatening to Chinese territory, regional interests, and global access.

As we will see, Chinese writings on this matter do not provide clear evidence of intent to wrest control of the Western Pacific from the United States and its fleet.[8] Defending mainland China and preventing U.S. intervention in the event of conflict over Taiwan have thus far been the most explicit purposes declared by the Chinese. Yet the requirements of even these limited objectives are causing the Chinese to extend the reach of their naval and anti-naval forces farther and farther into the Pacific, at least to the so-called First Island Chain.[9] In addition, China has displayed a willingness to use naval force to

---

8 Daniel M. Hartnett and Frederic Vellucci, "Toward a Maritime Security Strategy: An Analysis of Chinese Views Since the Early 1990s," in Saunders et al., eds., 2011, pp. 81–108.

9 The First Island Chain is the southern tip of Japan through the Philippines. The Second Island Chain includes Japan, Marianas, and Guam.

back its claims in disputes over territorial demarcations and maritime rights.[10] By implication, American sea denial will not be tolerable to China in the Western Pacific's nearest and most important waters: the South China Sea, the East China Sea, and the Yellow Sea. By further implication, China may be moving, albeit slowly, toward a posture of sea denial in the Western Pacific, which would be equally unacceptable to the United States. Assured access of U.S. shipping and naval forces to East Asian waters is as important as it has ever been.

Even in their boldest formulations, the Chinese see naval ambition and competition mainly in regional terms.[11] Chinese strategists and leaders have not articulated a commitment to, or even a firm grasp of, sea power in the classical sense. Unlike Great Britain, the United States, Imperial Germany, and Imperial Japan, China has not elevated sea strategy to the level of grand strategy—that is, so essential to national well-being and world standing as to warrant building and operating a blue-water fleet with strike power and transoceanic reach. But China may be drawn in this direction as its access to the world's commodities, markets, and thus oceans grows in strategic importance. Beyond trade, the increasing value and expected abundance of resources in and under the seas have added another incentive to gain and use sea power—whether competitively or collaboratively is unclear—especially for rapidly developing economies such as China and its East Asian neighbors. For these reasons, rather than be dissuaded if the United States seeks to remain dominant in the Western Pacific, the Chinese could be all the more determined to break that dominance.

Whether China sprints or sidles toward sea-power status and strategy, it is yet to be seen whether and when it can organize the requisite operational capabilities. Modern China is a land power, not a "seafaring nation" in the mold of the United States, Great Britain, and formerly Japan, Spain, and France.[12] Even if ample resources and tech-

---

[10] In fairness to China, other East Asian states, e.g., Japan, Vietnam, and the Philippines, have also dispatched naval vessels on occasion to back up their claims.

[11] Hartnett and Vellucci, 2011.

[12] Others deserving of the description of a seafaring nation include Portugal, Australia, Chile, the Netherlands, and Norway.

nology are applied, there are requisites of doctrine, expertise, seamanship, and safety to meet. Sea power must be institutionalized, not just constructed. Naval "hardware" is no better than the "software" that runs it, at sea and at home. It took Imperial Germany, another emerging land power, from roughly 1880 to 1914 to marshal the know-how and confidence to confront British sea power (and even then without success).[13] That the Soviet Union, despite massive investment, never seriously challenged American sea control in the Pacific or Atlantic illustrates the difficulty a great land power faces in operating naval forces against more seasoned sea powers. China faces many hurdles—naval architecture, integrating new technology, underway-replenishment skills, basing options, and able sailors, from deckhands to admirals—that will take a generation or more to overcome, especially if it means to have a blue-water navy of its own.

Yet, acquiring sea power, and being a sea power, does not necessarily mean having and using power *upon the sea*. Theory, as we will see, suggests that sea power is the ability to exert power over what occurs at sea—or power *of the sea*. When those theories were offered in the 19th century, extant technology and capabilities made power upon the sea—notably, grand battle fleets—necessary if not sufficient to have power of the sea. Nowadays, power from elsewhere—under the sea, over the sea, from land, from space, and through "cyber-space"—can be used to exert sea denial, if not to maintain sea control. Thus, even with no grand fleet, presently or eventually, China (and others) can have sea power. Indeed, it is China's current commitment to *anti*-naval capabilities, sea-based and otherwise, that make our topic more urgent than waiting to see whether China builds a blue-water navy. By proper definition, China is already creating sea power and challenging American sea power, whether or not it tries to replicate U.S. naval forces.

Likewise, how the United States responds to this Chinese challenge may involve forms of sea power unlike the naval forces on which it has relied and relies today. While the *forms* of both Chinese and U.S. sea power in the Western Pacific may be untraditional, the *purposes* will

---

13 Peter M. Swartz, "Rising Powers and Naval Powers," in Saunders et al., eds., 2011, pp. 1–22.

essentially be those that have motivated sea powers traditionally: to assure or deny access for shipping and navies. As the Chinese consider how best to gain sea power, it is important that today's naval force not be an anchor on American thinking.

Even as China becomes a sea power, in familiar or new ways, history indicates that Sino-American naval rivalry and conflict are not inevitable. The cases of Great Britain and Germany before World War I and of the United States and Japan before World War II show that naval competition can end in hostilities. But the case of Great Britain and the United States in the late 1800s suggests that an established and a rising sea power may evolve into co-existence, cooperation, and even, when confronted by common enemies, alliance. If the past is a guide, it is a mix of entangled interests, relative naval strength, and competitive hubris that determines whether sea powers collide or collaborate.

Technological Change

Today's U.S. Navy has powerful offensive naval capabilities. In contrast, given its current aims and limitations, China is concentrating on defensive, or anti-naval, capabilities. Again, technology is fundamentally altering the relationship between offense and defense, and thus between denial and control of the sea. In particular, improvements in targeting are posing increasingly severe threats to surface vessels within range of new sensors and weapons. Consequently, naval strength, which has historically been equated with surface warships, may be trumped by anti-surface capabilities, such as long-range missiles guided from space against targets tracked from space. In response, the key capabilities in sea power may soon shift from surface fleets to capabilities under and above the seas, as well as drones. Compounding these new developments is the prospect that sea power will be endangered or even redefined by cyber power, targeting computerized command and control systems. Already, concentrated battle-fleets are being replaced by distributed networks of ships and sensors, at once necessitated by the vulnerability and enabled by the networking that information technology provides.

While the U.S. Navy is grappling with the effects of these technological changes, it could be an even bigger challenge for Chinese naval forces, given China's inexperience and U.S. advantages in targeting. Even if China is determined and able to become a sea power, it may discover that traditional surface forces, acquired at great cost in money and time, are not survivable—and perhaps not necessary. From their writings and investments, we know the Chinese are aware of the implications of advances in targeting and networking: They are exploiting these very technologies to threaten the U.S. surface fleet in the Western Pacific. The impact of long-range precision-guided weapons is a consideration that will weigh both on the Chinese as they decide how to pursue sea power and on the Americans as they decide how to maintain sea power in the Western Pacific.

The particular problem of sea denial in the Western Pacific is a subset of a larger challenge faced by the United States, given its general reliance on power projection to and throughout this distant region. The Chinese are employing a variety of technologies to achieve what in strategic jargon are called "anti-access" (A2) and "area-denial" (AD) capabilities with missiles, air, naval, anti-satellite, and cyber-war weapon systems. (Hereafter, A2 + AD = A2AD—now a popular military acronym.) U.S. air bases, facilities, and land forces stationed in or dispatched to the region are also becoming more vulnerable. However, because U.S. sea power figures centrally in U.S. strategy, influence, and possible operations in the Western Pacific, it is with this particular vulnerability that this study deals.

Thus, technology is changing and even revolutionizing how we conceive sea power, sea denial, and sea control. It is making important the distinction between power of the sea and power upon the sea. Presently, it is shifting the balance between defense and offense at sea in favor of the former, making control harder and denial easier. Technology also means that rival sea powers of the 21st century, unlike those of the 19th and 20th, need not and most likely will not try to mimic each other's naval forces in kind or size. The response of Imperial Germany to British sea power was to build a High Seas Fleet that could challenge the Royal Navy by resembling the Royal Navy: After all, it took battleships to sink battleships, until submarines and airplanes entered the picture. Likewise, Imperial Japan and the United States each built more and more, and bigger and bigger, aircraft carriers as the best and perhaps only sure way of neutralizing the other's aircraft carriers. Now, by reducing the importance of proximity of forces, technology—notably sensor, missile, and global communications technology—is superseding such same-for-same linkage.

It follows that competition between rising and established sea powers, like China and the United States, will probably be asymmetrical, though not necessarily less heated than the naval arms races of old. Apostles of American sea power would be unwise to take great comfort in the fact that China is not building a large carrier fleet—and unwise to take great comfort in the large carrier fleet the United States can deploy in the Western Pacific.

The Oceanic Commons

Just as technology is changing the nature of sea power, globalization is changing its assumptions. Relationships between states with powerful fleets, or between established and rising powers, have been largely competitive since the era of mercantilism and competing imperial ambitions—indeed, since ancient times. As we will argue, economic integration and dramatic growth in sea-borne trade have made the oceans a "commons" of an interdependent world. All who depend on these commons share an interest in uninterrupted and unthreatened flows of energy fuels, raw materials, parts, and goods. The growth of direct overseas investment, multinational production, interwoven supply chains, and declining self-sufficiency makes it counterproductive to interfere with the sea-borne trade of other nations, which historically has been a strong motivation for sea power. Whether common interests in maritime security will supersede competitive, distrustful impulses could be a pivotal issue in the relationship of U.S. and Chinese sea power.

If any major country has benefited more from global economic integration than the United States, it is China. World trade has enabled China to expand production far beyond what domestic demand would justify, which has in turn created the industrial and technological capacities to allow China to be a major sea power, whatever form that may take. Yet, globalization has also given rise to non-state actors, such as pirates and terrorists, who might interrupt these flows or else traffic by sea in drugs, humans, fighters, weapons, and other illicit cargoes. Likewise, rogue states, with or without traditional navies, might use new technologies and daring tactics to disrupt or misuse the maritime commons. This has caused the United States, notwithstanding its naval superiority, increasingly to stress collective maritime security, as we will see.[14]

China, too, has much to gain from such cooperation, even if it means collaborating with U.S. naval forces to protect maritime interests that it and the United States share. Thus, even as China and the United States may be drawn toward competitive sea power, they may also be drawn toward cooperative sea power. If it were not for great-power politics and mistrust, China might elect to rely on American sea power to patrol and keep open the sea-lanes on which it depends. Keep in mind that until the late 19th century, when American leaders determined that global ambition demanded sea power, the United States depended on the Royal Navy to maintain maritime security, even in the Western Hemisphere. Although there is no explicit indication that the Chinese prefer to "free ride" on U.S. worldwide naval dominance, they are in fact a beneficiary of the security that the U.S. Navy provides along oil-supply routes from the Persian Gulf to East Asia. Moreover, if China rejects maritime cooperation, perhaps out of distrust of the United States, it may encourage even closer cooperation between the United States and others, including two other naval powers, Japan and India. While the Chinese might believe that these others will side with the United States anyway, some in China are concerned about its isolation.

If China were to cooperate with and, by implication, depend on American sea power, it would risk being disadvantaged if cooperation

[14] Admiral Mike Mullen, Chief of Naval Operations, "A Global Network of Nations for a Free and Secure Maritime Commons," speech at Naval War College, Newport, R.I., September 2005.

breaks down and the United States uses its sea power to contain and deny China access. Does China want to gamble on U.S. acceptance of the Kantian logic of common security, even as U.S. capabilities permit it instead to follow the Hobbesian logic of raw power?

Geo-Politics

Interest in common maritime security may be on the rise, but it has not replaced sea-power politics. In both China and the United States, there is plenty of doubt about the other's true calculations and intentions: Is China content to see the United States remain the dominant sea power in the Western Pacific? Probably not. Might the United States take advantage of its sea dominance to threaten injury to Chinese interests in a crisis? Presumably. Would China exploit a decline of U.S. sea power to increase its influence over East Asia? Likely. Would the United States regard growing Chinese naval capabilities as a contribution to common maritime security? Almost certainly not. Would either regard the other's sea power as interchangeable with its own in confronting threats to common interests? Emphatically not. In short, the Western Pacific is and will remain an oceanic space in which the world's two strongest powers each view the other's presence as potentially inimical.

One of the most important features of geo-politics in the Western Pacific is that these two powers are not alone. A tenet of sea-power theory has been to ally with friendly states that augment naval capabilities or provide bases and welcoming ports.[15] The United States enjoys close political and security relations with some capable mid-level Asian naval powers, such as Japan, Australia, and now India. The harder China presses its maritime claims and ambitions, the more these and other East Asians will look to the United States and its navy. This is already becoming a countervailing factor—politically, at least—for the growing strength of China, whose assertiveness in recent years has reju-

---

15 Alfred T. Mahan, *Naval Strategy: Compared and Contrasted with the Principles and Practice of Military Operations on Land*, London: Sampson Low, Marston, and Company, 1911, pp. 118–131.

venated U.S. alliances that enable and supplement U.S. sea power from Northeast Asia to the Indian Ocean.

In addition, the United States and China themselves are susceptible to shifting geo-political pressures that could affect their respective commitments to sea power in the Western Pacific. Just as the United States turned its strategic orientation from Europe during the Cold War to the Middle East in the post-9/11 decade and lately to the Pacific, it could turn again. For example, if the Persian Gulf fell under threat from Iran, U.S. military options would rest on naval, as well as land-based, air-strike capabilities. Barring another massive U.S. defense build-up, this could divert forces, resources, and attention from the Western Pacific, leaving China less vulnerable and perhaps bolder.

China's shift from an ancient land power to would-be sea power has been a part of a larger strategic swivel from its rivalries and conflicts with Russia and India to its push to challenge U.S. predominance at least around Taiwan and potentially in the wider Western Pacific. This too could change. Suspicions between China and India simmer, even if their border disputes have been put on the back burner by both countries.[16] Although India has more immediate concerns with Pakistan and militants affiliated with it, and China is preoccupied with the United States, Sino-Indian tensions could flare again as a result of hegemonic competition or deadly incidents that fuel persistent animosities. Less likely but not excluded is the onset of Sino-Russian confrontation over resource-rich Asiatic Russia, where Chinese migration and investment are weakening Moscow's grip. Yet, even the resumption of troubles with its land neighbors would not cause China to view U.S. sea power in the Western Pacific with equanimity, especially if the United States and India formed an encircling anti-Chinese alliance. Recall that Imperial Germany had its own land adversaries when it launched its effort to end Britain's sea dominance.

If there is a flaw in established sea-power theory, it is the failure to recognize that the quest of sea power by one state can stimulate a similar quest by another, and so on in a costly spiral of worsening maritime insecurity for both. Great Britain's policy of maintaining naval

---

[16] *The Economist*, "Smoke Without Fire?" June 2–8, 2012, p. 54.

strength equivalent to the sum of any other two powers' naval strength did not dissuade Germany from mounting a major challenge: quite the opposite. Likewise, Imperial Japan's effort to have sea power second to none in the Pacific led to a major expansion of the U.S. Navy in the late 1930s. In both cases, the urge for sea power caused competition, fanned antagonism, and helped bring on war.

Is competition the dominant dynamic in the case of China and the United States? Or could it be attenuated and even replaced by an appreciation that maritime partnership in the region would leave both China and the United States more secure at lower risk, lower cost, and friendlier relations? After all, Chinese and American ships cooperate, if warily, to protect shipping from Somali pirates in the Gulf of Aden. In East Asia, however, the Chinese have been cool and coy to U.S. overtures in such a direction, though this may not be a reason for the United States to abandon the idea.

In sum, changes wrought by global economic integration, technological change, China's growing power, and shifting U.S. and Chinese geo-strategic orientations might or might not point toward the sort of collision between sea powers modern history has seen. It depends on choices made by U.S. and Chinese political leaders.

Geography

The future of sea power, like the history and study of sea power, is to a very large degree a function of geography. The importance of sea-based trade, the possibility of securing and disrupting this trade, the ability to extract sea-based resources, the concentration and movements of naval forces, and, of course, ease of oceanic access all depend on it. Relative sea power, and thus rivalry between established and rising sea powers, is both driven and constrained by geography. Japan enjoyed an advantage over Great Britain and the United States in seeking to control the Western Pacific, as did (and does) the United States over all others in the waters of the Western Hemisphere. As true world sea powers, both Britain and America overcame the problem of distance by building and operating multi-ocean navies.

Geography also determines whether passage is easy and safe, or not. Germany required access to colonies, resources, and markets through the North Atlantic, which meant passage through the confines of the British-patrolled North Sea. Geography forced the Soviet navy to transit narrow waters largely controlled by the United States and its allies (Norway, Denmark, the UK, Turkey, and Japan) in order to reach open ocean. "Like Germany, the Soviet Union would find its fleets bottled up in a major conflict, while those already at sea would become hostages to fortune."[17] All else being equal, powers with several wide paths to multiple seas have an advantage—thus, island powers such as Great Britain and Japan, as well as a two-ocean power like the United States.[18]

Geography obviously affects American and Chinese sea power in the Western Pacific. At first glance, the United States appears to be disadvantaged by the distances its navy must travel to get to and operate in the Western Pacific. Thus, naval nuclear propulsion, at which the U.S. Navy excels, enables its carriers and submarines to reach and remain at sea virtually anywhere; but nuclear propulsion is also a constraint—an expensive one at that, given the cost of such engineering plants. However, America's apparent geographical disadvantages have been attenuated by the presence of reliable regional allies with deep-water harbors, modern facilities, and good navies of their own. In the Western Pacific, Japan, Australia, the Philippines, Singapore, and other allies largely offset the problem of distance, and will thus remain critical to American sea power and interests in the region. In addition, of course, the homeland security afforded by the North Atlantic and Pacific Oceans has long been and will remain a major U.S. advantage, unless and until technology reduces the difficulty adversaries face in threatening American soil (as has already occurred with respect to strategic nuclear weapons and is occurring with respect to cyber-war).

---

[17] Observation from James Dobbins of RAND.

[18] Russia (and previously the Soviet Union) has been unable to turn its continental size into a sea-power advantage because of limitations on ice-free basing and the need to pass through tight choke-points in all directions.

Generally speaking, China has the opposite of U.S. advantages and disadvantages as far as the Western Pacific is concerned. Being on the Western Pacific, its naval forces as well as shipping in and out of China are close enough to receive at least some protection from the mainland. Insofar as its main maritime security interests are in the waters of the region, its need for a blue-water fleet, both expensive and vulnerable, is reduced. Moreover, it can use land-based sensors and weapons to track and, if need be, strike U.S. vessels in the Western Pacific, giving it sea-denial options that do not depend on traditional high-seas naval forces.

But a look at the map reminds us—surely reminds the Chinese—that geography is not an unambiguous blessing for China (any more than the vastness of the Atlantic and Pacific are an unambiguous blessing for the United States). China has three geographic problems. First, its territory is exposed, by virtue of proximity, to threats from U.S. sea-based strike power in the Western Pacific. Unless and until China has the ability to maintain a comparable naval presence as close to the United States as U.S. naval presence is to China—or develops sensors and conventional weapons of transoceanic range, which are decades away at the soonest—it must live with this disparity.

China's second geographic problem is nearly as noticeable on the map. To reach the high seas that its fleets and shipping need to cross for access to world markets and resources—the Pacific and Indian Oceans—they must pass through relatively tight waters crowded with islands and countries that may not be sympathetic to China in crises or war. Chinese control of the South China Sea, East China Sea, and Yellow Sea is a daunting challenge, not to mention unacceptable to the United States and others. Beyond these waters, China's access to the Pacific and Indian Oceans involves running a gauntlet of straits and other choke-points patrolled by U.S. forces. Small wonder that Chinese strategists tend to see access to the world and its oceans in much the same way late-19th-century Germans did: not as welcoming expanses but as harrowing narrows.

The intricate geography of the Western Pacific is even more disadvantageous to China when taking into account that most of the other states of the region are allies of the United States or, if not allies, at least looking to the United States for security in the face of China's growing strength. Maybe the United States will allow long-standing alliances to decay or fail to develop new security relationships; but it seems at present determined to avoid just that. Conversely, perhaps China will earn the deference of its neighbors from Northeast to Southeast Asia; but it seems at present more likely that its growing military and naval capabilities—its A2AD and coastal fleets—will have the opposite effect. The starting point, by virtue of the path history has taken, is that the United States has the advantage of strong allies and expanding relationships, which in turn mitigates its geographic liabilities and aggravates China's. As long as the United States maintains it presence and influence, including its sea power, in the region, China may be inclined to remedy this strategic problem by tacking away from rivalry and toward cooperation at sea. In that case, U.S. interests in the Western Pacific could be protected without having to confront a challenge to U.S. sea power.

This introduction requires one further clarification: What is meant by "Western Pacific"? Narrowly defined, the Western Pacific is just that, and thus does not include the South China Sea, East China Sea, Yellow Sea, or other important bodies of water that wash against China and other countries in East Asia. China might be more relaxed about U.S. sea power in the Western Pacific if the U.S. Navy did not frequent the seas adjacent to China. But of course, the U.S. Navy does frequent those seas, which are more critical and more contested than the Pacific beyond them. While U.S. and Chinese sea power, including anti-naval power, might eventually vie for control of the entire Pacific, Indian, and other great oceans, the waters where maritime competition—or, perhaps, cooperation—will be most intense in the next decade or so are those near China. For our purposes, we will consider them to be parts, and perhaps the most important parts, of what is broadly called the Western Pacific.

Structure

This book is about the strategic choices that American and Chinese decisionmakers face, shaped by geography, history, technology, economics, and politics. It is structured according to the factors likely to determine whether China will feel compelled to challenge U.S. sea power and interests in the Western Pacific and what the United States can and should do about it. Chapter Two reviews the theory and history of sea power, including lessons from notable past rivalries and how they ended. Its point of departure—port of embarkation, if you will—is the work of American naval theorist Alfred Thayer Mahan (1840–1914), whose reflections on sea power and history shaped naval strategy, capabilities, relations, and conflicts to come.[19] Theory and history provide the scenery for how Americans and Chinese may act out such ideas as sea control, sea denial, global reach, concentrated naval power, safeguarding versus severing sea lines of communication, and offense versus defense.

As ranges of accurate weapons have increased by orders of magnitude—from a few miles for gunnery to thousands of miles for missiles—the particulars of past naval rivalries and battles become less germane. Yet, the point is not that the modern history of sea power will furnish definitive answers to the case of China and the United States, but that it may provide clues about how one power's leaders will view and react to the other. By the end of the book, we will see which lessons from the theory and experience of sea power apply to the Sino-U.S. case despite technological change.

---

[19] The view that Mahan was the father of sea power theory is not universally held. In *For the Common Defense: A Military History of the United States from 1607 to 2012* (New York: Free Press, 2012), Allan Millet, Peter Maslowksi, and William Feis argue that Mahan mainly summed up somewhat earlier work by Admiral David Dixon Porter and Stephen D. Luce, though with the "advantages of writing eloquently and at the moment when imperialism and navalism were in full flower." Further, Mahan was in the thrall of British sea dominance and therefore did not understand the dynamics and consequences of rivalry. Finally, he did not appreciate the importance of technology or anticipate that it would call into question some of his ideas. This author considers these criticisms to be not entirely unfair. The intent is not to exalt Mahan but to refer to ideas that were as much his as anyone's to illuminate more recent and prospective developments concerning sea power.

Chapter Three analyzes current and prospective U.S. and Chinese interests in the Western Pacific, Asia, and the world, insofar as they bear on sea power. How the United States and China assess each other's capabilities and intentions, and thus set their own requirements, will be affected by how they perceive both divergent and convergent interests. Despite their interdependence and relatively compatible current global outlooks, contradictions between U.S. presence and Chinese aims in the region point toward the possibility of intense and potentially dangerous competition. This chapter will consider both American and Chinese perspectives and prospects regarding sea power.

Chapter Four deals with the effects of technological change. As both powers seek to master and incorporate the technologies of the information revolution, sea power will have to adjust to the growing vulnerability of surface fleets and the roles of anti-naval, undersea, unmanned, space, and cyber-war capabilities. With advanced targeting making surface forces less survivable and with advanced networking offering options to distribute forces, sea denial may get easier and sea control harder. The technologies being used to improve naval and anti-naval capabilities are largely based on commercial technologies that are propelled by and spread through global markets. As China grows increasingly competitive in those markets, lasting U.S. advantages in applying technology to solve operational sea-power challenges cannot be assured or assumed. The United States holds cards it can yet play to slow the effects of Chinese advances, but it will have to play a more daring game than established sea powers or the U.S. Navy itself usually does.

Chapter Five considers prospects for regional cooperation in providing maritime security. Japan, India, South Korea, Australia, and key Southeast Asian states have strong interests in how American and Chinese naval strategies and capabilities develop and interact. Insofar as China is perceived as eroding U.S. naval dominance and political resolve, other regional actors could become more accommodating toward China and its claims in regional waters, even leading to a Chinese sphere of influence prejudicial to U.S. interests. Alternatively, under U.S. leadership, these states could form a maritime-security coalition, which China could be invited to join.

Chapter Six offers conclusions about sea power in the Western Pacific in the coming two decades, based on theory and history, U.S. and Chinese interests, the course of technology, and the positions of others in the region. It suggests necessary changes in the forms of American sea power and a way to advance U.S. interests without wasteful competition and dangerous confrontation.

Both East Asia and sea power are of great and growing importance to world progress and U.S. interests. Yet both are entering periods of uncertainty and discontinuity. For the United States, the status quo has been comfortable but is not sustainable: The United States cannot dictate the path and use of technology any more than it can contain the rise of China. "Steady-as-you-go"—the order that has served regional stability and U.S. interests since World War II—has run its course. The United States faces tough choices that require bold decisions.

CHAPTER TWO

Theory and Lessons of History

"If navies, as all agree, exist for the protection of commerce, it inevitably follows that in war they must aim at depriving their enemy of that great resource."—A. T. Mahan[1]

Factors of Sea Power

Sea power is the product of economics, politics, technology, and geography: necessitated by economics, textured by politics, enabled by technology, and shaped by geography. From international economics comes the need to transit the oceans safely and predictably. From international politics come confrontations and hostilities that may prompt nations to interfere with other nations' sea-borne trade, giving rise to the need for navies.[2] Domestic politics allow naval officers, business interests, and politicians to advocate, machinate, and formulate the particulars of sea power. Technology, defined to include the skill and ingenuity of people, can determine the balance between offense and defense, as well as the capabilities that afford the greatest operational advantages. If technology is equally accessible, the amount of resources a nation commits to naval capabilities determines its sea power. Geography, while largely beyond the control of nations, can make them more or less vulnerable and more or less able to project sea power where needed.

---

1 Alfred T. Mahan, *The Interest of America in Sea Power, Present and Future*, London: Sampson Low, Marston, and Company, 1897, p. 128.

2 Mahan derived the importance of sea power from the economic need for unchallenged use of the seas and the strategic value of challenging an adversary's use of the seas. John B. Hattendorf, ed., *Mahan on Naval Strategy: Selections from the Writings of Rear Admiral Alfred Thayer Mahan*, Annapolis, Md.: Naval Institute Press, 1991.

Sea-power theory is about how these factors combine in competition and conflict. It was born of the great-power naval competitions of the 19th century and earlier, and in turn it influenced 20th-century war and peace. As elegant as the theory may seem, it originated in a world very different from ours. Thus, any merit there is in trying to apply to the 21st century the theory and history of the 19th and 20th depends on how the factors of sea power—economics, politics, and technology—have changed. The extent and effects of such change are the underlying analytic questions of this book.

Global economic integration has greatly expanded international trade and investment across regions, making sea transport more important. In addition to commerce, the seas have become more coveted and contested because of raw materials beneath them and thus the question of who owns or controls them. Ravenous appetites for energy, minerals, and food among rapidly developing and developed countries alike have made ocean exploitation more economical—in fact, lucrative enough to risk conflict. In East Asian waters, estimated resource concentrations have huge economic implications for numerous countries with contradictory claims and have opened a new front for competition.

At the same time, globalization may attenuate geo-political rivalry insofar as one nation's success depends on that of others. If all powers can prosper from trade that depends on international tranquility in which trade can grow, it is harder for any of them to justify violating that tranquility for unilateral gain. Globalization can also reinforce shared interests in secure trade, making confrontation between sea powers less likely. As we will see, contradictions between globalization and great-power rivalry are evident in the case of Sino-U.S. relations and in the role that sea power plays in those relations.

The domestic politics of sea power seems to have changed very little since the 19th century: Special interests in navies are as active as ever. In Washington and Beijing today, admirals, industrialists, and politicians are not motivated to downplay the other power's capabilities, though they lack the influence of naval advocates in London, Berlin, Tokyo, and Washington a hundred years ago. In contrast, technology has gone through several revolutions since then, most of which bear on sea power: aviation, missilery, nuclear power, digital networking, and high-resolution sensing. Thus, the concept of sea power was formed in a specific 19th-century context, important aspects of which no longer obtain.

That context was one of rivalry—economic, imperial, and military—among nation-states. While weak states had ample reason to fear stronger ones, it was the possibility of conflict between great powers, thus their peacetime pecking order and behavior in crises, that ordered world affairs. After Napoleon, Europe's great powers endeavored to avoid war by managing their relations in variable alliances that brought both national advantage and international equilibrium; or so they thought. Still, they were rivals, and as such they saw one another's military forces as potentially dangerous. While the great-power system survived for 100 years, when it disintegrated in horrific violence, war-making capacity—increasingly mechanized—was the currency of both rivalries and alliances, as well as the backdrop of world affairs.

As Mahan put it, "[U]pon organized force the world so far has progressed and still progresses. Upon organized force depends the extended shield, under which the movements of peace advance in quietness."[3] For all his ideas about how to wage war, Mahan himself expected, and hoped, that great-power warfare's growing destructive potential would make it less likely or at least more restrained. He died in 1914 before World War I would demolish his hope. In fact, the sea power Mahan prescribed combined with the power-politics he assumed to produce the conflict he dreaded.

With trade expanding, grand navies were putatively threatening. Implicit in Great Britain's strategy of maintaining an outsized fleet was the intent to deny to other powers the maritime prerogatives the British were determined to maintain for themselves. As captured in the quotation at the beginning of this chapter, fleets were essentially dual-purpose: able both to protect and to sever economic lifelines. A strong navy was inherently *strategic* in that it implied a threat to strangle a rival. Thus, an established great power, e.g., Britain, required naval strength to maintain its strategic advantage, as rising powers, e.g., the

---

[3] Alfred T. Mahan, *Some Neglected Aspects of War*, Boston: Little, Brown and Company, 1907, p. 89, quoted in Hattendorf, 1991.

United States and Germany, sought it to eliminate their strategic disadvantage. Vying for advantage occurred even as commerce was expanding. (Keep in mind that trade also had a competitive aspect, based on the mercantilist belief that one country could prosper most at the expense of others.) The premise of sea power was distrust between great powers, notwithstanding their trade. Industrialization added both to the economic criticality of maritime trade and to the naval capability to disrupt it.

Today's established great power and rising great power—the United States and China—seem to distrust each other enough not to let their economic lifelines, critical waters and, in China's case, coasts go undefended, or to eschew naval rivalry in favor of naval collaboration. Indeed, naval competition is now heating up in East Asia, a region that owes decades of strong economic growth to trade. Simply put, the United States regards sea control as essential to its economic and security interests in East Asia, and China is no less adamant that U.S. sea control threatens Chinese interests and even Chinese territory. If the world's most important relationship, in some of the world's most important waters, is being shaped by goals of sea control and fears of sea denial, the theory and lessons of sea power are worth learning.

Bearing in mind limits on the value of lessons from a bygone world, this chapter will examine the theory of sea power as it arose in the late 19th century, as well as three cases where economics and geopolitics combined to cause competitive surges in naval capabilities: that between Great Britain and the United States (roughly 1880–1895), that between Great Britain and Germany (1890–1914), and that between the United States and Japan (1930–1941). In each case, an established sea power (Great Britain, Great Britain again, and the United States) was perceived by a rising one (the United States, Germany, and Japan, respectively) as having the means and presumed intent to frustrate its aspirations, throttle its economy, and even threaten it directly. Yet the cases differ in their causes, in the interests of their protagonists, and in their outcomes. The chapter concludes by drawing lessons for the Sino-American case from these cases and from the theory behind them.

Sea Power Then and Now

The concept of sea power gained both definition and prominence as the West's colonial powers began to industrialize in the second half of the 19th century. Control of and access to empires was thought by many to become more critical as Britain, France, Germany and others developed manufacturing and built railroads, creating a hunger for fuels, ores, and other materials.[4] In turn, these European states came to rely heavily on overseas markets for their manufactures, which allowed domestic production to exceed domestic demand, thus spurring growth. Broadly speaking, world economic development was ignited by industrialization and international commerce (and has continued since, except for world war and depression). It is estimated that global per capita gross domestic product (GDP) grew negligibly from the 11th century until the mid–19th century, then grew by 300 percent by the end of the 19th century, then by 900 percent during the 20th century.[5] Thus, the most significant progress in human material conditions has coincided with expanded use of the world's water "highways," as Mahan called them. With industrialization, oceanic trade graduated from spices and vices to goods and resources essential to economic success. With its natural blessings, under-utilized geographic expanse, swelling immigration and population, and growing domestic demand, the United States was later than the European powers to develop the need for resources, markets, or a strong navy.

Despite growing trade among them, the European powers were naval competitors. Size mattered: both of multi-ocean fleets and of the economies needed to build, maintain, and operate them. The Netherlands, Portugal, and Spain could no longer keep pace with Great Britain and France, and their possessions shrank correspondingly. In contrast, newly unified Germany could catch up and keep up, and its possessions expanded correspondingly. Industrialization enabled those still

---

4 It is true that two of the fastest growing economies of the late 19th century—Germany and Japan—had no overseas possessions. In both cases, however, industrialization led to increased interest in overseas resources, markets, and possessions, as well as in sea power.

5 Lawrence J. Broz, "The U.S. and the World Economy in the 19th Century," February 2012.

in the game to construct larger, faster, and less sinkable steel-armored ships propelled by steam power and equipped with increasingly accurate long-range guns. Great Britain—first to industrialize, with the largest empire and greatest dependence on imports and markets—led in naval capabilities, which motivated old adversaries France and the United States and future adversary Germany to follow suit. Emerging from isolation, undergoing rapid industrialization, and in growing need of materials and markets, Japan was close behind.

It was at this time that American naval officer, professor, and strategist Alfred Thayer Mahan offered lessons, theories, requirements, and implications of sea power. His fame and impact came as the United States turned its attention from post–Civil War recovery and continental expansion to global potential. Mahan's political champions had conquests and empire in their sights.[6] More than that, they wanted war: if not with Britain (disliked by them but strong) then with Spain (disliked and weak). While Mahan did not share their martial gusto, he was as unabashed as they in believing that the United States could and must become a world power. Mahan formulated in writings and teachings (and Roosevelt then retailed in corridors of power) the idea that the key to greatness, fortune, empire, and military success was sea power. In essence, sea power was both a prerequisite and a manifestation of national greatness, as Great Britain demonstrated in Mahan's world.

American sea power, thus world power, was but a gleam in Mahan's eye when he began his work (1884). His theories were informed by his reading of history from Roman to modern times, but rooted deeply in the 19th century's prime example: the Royal Navy and its indispensable role in enabling Britain's new economic model and commanding its empire. In the words of Robert Massie:

> The Victorian Age, *Pax Britannica*, Splendid Isolation, the Empire on Which the Sun Never Sets, existed because "Britannia Ruled the Waves." Essentially, she ruled unchallenged. Former

---

[6] Evan Thomas, *The War Lovers: Roosevelt, Lodge, Hearst, and the Rush to Empire, 1898*, New York: Little, Brown and Company, 2010.

> antagonists, the Spanish and the Dutch, had no navies to speak of; Russia and the United States were deeply engaged in consolidating control over their own landmasses; the German Empire did not exist.

Although its old enemy, France, had the world's second largest fleet, "Great Britain's naval supremacy remained unshaken."[7]

Mahan's theory flowed from his observation that the 19th century's greatest power was its greatest sea power. What Great Britain had practiced, Mahan articulated: Because sea power can deliver national economic success and strategic advantage, it warrants the national commitment that it requires. In the British case, growing commercial and financial strength "enabled the country to adequately fund outsized naval fleets, and those fleets protected the trade and achieved the victories that enabled the British economy to flourish."[8] Mahan noticed that Britain had peers (France, for instance) in all categories of power save one: sea power. It was their superiority at sea that enabled the British to excel in exploiting industrial technology, in expanding production (well beyond domestic demand), and in securing access to the world's abundance of raw materials. This implied that sea power was the sine qua non for world power and strategic advantage. Indeed, Britain's navy made it the superpower of the 19th century. Knowing this, British leaders built and followed a national strategy based on sea power, and they saw to it that the Royal Navy would get the resources it needed to remain supreme.

To Mahan, the heart of sea power was the *offensive potency of a concentrated fleet.* This was consistent with his belief that the "first principle of warfare is concentration—drawing force together at the centers which for the moment are important."[9] But his concept was much larger than concentrated offensive naval power, encompassing

---

7 Robert K. Massie, *Dreadnought: Britain, Germany, and the Coming of the Great War*, New York: Ballantine, 1991, p. 373.

8 Swartz, 2011.

9 Alfred T. Mahan, *Lessons of the War with Spain and Other Articles*, Boston: Little, Brown and Company, 1899, p. 258, quoted in Hattendorf, 1991.

geography, navigation, economics, demographics, culture, and politics. Mahan both traced and predicted how sea power influences "history," by which he meant the rise and fall of powers, the gain and loss of possessions, the ability to rule in peace, and the means to prevail in war. His line of thinking went like this:

- To succeed economically and grow strong strategically, a nation needs to industrialize and produce more than it consumes.
- Production requires more raw materials than the nation has.
- Trade—importing materials and exporting products—is therefore vital to national economic success.
- The oceans are the great highways of that trade.
- Use of the oceans is vital to any nation that relies on trade and aspires to succeed economically and strategically.
- The ability of a state to protect this use and to deny its enemy of it can determine the outcome of wars, competition over power, and international standing.
- While sea power is important for any state, it is crucial for those with the potential and goal to become world powers.
- The most effective measure in war at sea is to sever the enemy's sea lines of communication.
- The ability to destroy the enemy's fleet is crucial to assure this is achievable and should be the main goal of war.
- Offense is dominant; given offensive dominance, defense is needed only to enable offense.
- Speed is important, but not as important as concentrated force.
- Distance is a problem unless mitigated by bases and allies.
- Because battle fleets can only be defeated by battle fleets, the capabilities to control the seas are essentially the same as those to deny others such control.

For Mahan, sea power was power upon the *surface* of the seas—naturally enough given the state of technology. Submarines were novelties; aviation was science fiction; space satellites had not been imagined. Because communications were line-of-sight and gunnery ranges were at most a few miles, concentrated force necessitated concentrated fleets. Fleets were tethered to bases, even more so when coal replaced sail. Placing one's fleet between the enemy's fleet and its homeland was the key to victory.[10] Blockades, commerce raiding, and amphibious warfare were considered secondary to the "clash of battle fleets."[11]

Although sea power took a specific form in his mind's eye, Mahan's concepts were deeper and transcendent. Again, power *upon* the sea was essential because it was the way to attain power over what transpires *at* sea. While he did not anticipate the importance of submarines or contemplate aircraft carriers, he would have had no difficulty regarding them as inputs to sea power or amending his insistence on concentrated battle fleets to accommodate them. Long-range land-based anti-ship missiles would have been a greater shock to Mahan's thinking; but in the end, he would have admitted that they were part of the sea-power equation because they could visit offensive force upon navies and shipping. Even cyber-war can be fit into the purposes and essence of sea power as defined by Mahan. Looking back, the battleship formation expressed but did not define the concept of sea power. Looking ahead, naval forces will hardly be the only way to acquire and use sea power.

Mahan's work was both descriptive and prescriptive: He sought to persuade his own country's powers-that-be to commit to become the sea power that its size, location, ambitions, and seafaring ways implied it could be. He did battle not only with American apathy toward sea power but also with the idea that the fleet's purpose was to serve as the nation's "first line of defense"—a defense-mindedness that insulted three of his core beliefs: that the United States should be a global power, that global powers need navies less to guard their coasts than to safeguard their trade and prosperity, and that offense—the ability to disrupt another power's trade by first destroying its fleet—was the heart of sea power.

---

[10] The failure to get between the German High Seas Fleet and the safety of the German coast prevented the Royal Navy from turning a tactical victory into a strategic one in the Battle of Jutland. John Irving, *The Smoke Screen of Jutland*, New York: David McKay Company, 1966.

[11] Alfred T. Mahan, *Some Neglected Aspects of War*, p. 89, quoted in Hattendorf, 1991.

Upon publishing *The Influence of Sea Power upon History*, Mahan became hugely successful intellectually and politically—a strategic celebrity. His ideas rode a wave of national enthusiasm for world possessions, respect, and influence—based on claims of political, cultural, and racial (Anglo-Saxon) superiority, stirred by Roosevelt's "Americanism" and formulated in Lodge's "Large Policy."[12] From this moment, the U.S. Navy became synonymous with U.S. greatness (just as the Royal Navy meant British greatness). From 1890 to 1900, the U.S. fleet grew from 42 ships, of which 8 were steel and none were battleships, to 140 ships, of which 100 were steel and 8 were battleships.[13] In that decade, the Navy steamed past the U.S. Army in political influence and public esteem.

Roosevelt, Lodge, and Hearst favored war, not only for conquest but also to reinvigorate national spirit. Mahan demurred, arguing that deterrence is preferred to war, though it requires even greater naval predominance: "Force is never more operative than when it is known to exist but is not brandished."[14] On the whole—again, observing the Royal Navy during the 19th century—the greater the sea power, the less likely it had to be used.[15] Though Mahan supported the acquisition of colonies, his stress on offense was not meant to be a call to start wars, only to destroy enemy forces if war occurred. Mahan's concept was hijacked by others with a jingoistic fervor he did not share.

Though based on British experience and motivated by American ambition, Mahan's ideas "caused a global sensation."[16] In 1884, Kaiser Wilhelm wrote, "I am just now . . . devouring [*The Influence of Sea Power upon History*] and am trying to learn it by heart." He had it placed in the wardroom of every ship in the German fleet. The book was required reading in Japan's naval academy. Lodge and Roosevelt

---

[12] Thomas, 2010, Chapter Four.

[13] Naval History and Heritage Command, "U.S. Navy Active Ship Force Levels, 1886–Present," 2011.

[14] Alfred T. Mahan, *The Interest of America in International Conditions*, London: Sampson Low, Marston, and Company, 1910, p. 105, quoted in Hattendorf, 1991.

[15] The Royal Navy saw little action between the Napoleonic and First World Wars.

[16] Thomas, 2010.

regarded it as scripture: "Lodge would use Mahan as a preacher used the Bible."[17] Roosevelt, as Assistant Secretary of the Navy, leant Mahan's ideas political force, rhetorical thunder, and generous funding.[18]

The traction of Mahan's theory of sea power was badly weakened by World War I, which was mainly decided by land warfare (even between sea powers). The culminating Anglo-German naval battle, Jutland, ended in a tactical draw but a strategic win for Britain, which retained its mastery of the seas and consequent ability to gradually strangle the German economy and starve its population. Britain's blockade of Germany affected the war's course and outcome; but it also spurred development of the submarine to elude surface combatants and sink shipping. In general, World War I left losers and victors alike (except Japan) tired, broke, disinterested in more overseas possessions, and inclined to reduce, not increase, their fleets.

It was the railroad, another product of the industrial revolution, that was seen as enabling great land powers to consolidate control, compete, move troops, and determine the outcome of war, more so than control of the seas.[19] It was then that English geographer Halford Mackinder offered a competing and, considering World War I, more popular theory that land power, facilitated by rail transport, was the key to great power.[20] (Ironic that an Englishman fashioned the theory of land power while an American did so for sea power.) It took war in the Pacific between Japan and the United States two decades later to revive Mahan's theory of the importance of navies in war, peace, and history.

---

[17] Thomas, 2010, p. 72.

[18] Thomas, 2010.

[19] John Whiteclay Chambers II, ed., *The Oxford Companion to American Military History*, New York: Oxford University Press, 1999, pp. 720–721.

[20] Warning in 1918 that Germany's defeat did not end the danger it posed, Mackinder famously wrote: "Who rules East Europe commands the Heartland: Who rules the Heartland commands the World-Island: Who rules the World-Island commands the World." Quoted in John Halford Mackinder, *Democratic Ideals and Reality: A Study in the Politics of Reconstruction*, London: Constable and Company, 1919.

Half a century after Mahan, with the benefit of learning from the Japanese-American conflict, E. B. Potter and Admiral Chester Nimitz (retired commander of the U.S. Pacific Fleet in World War II) updated Mahan's ideas.[21] Based mainly on American naval success (something unknown to Mahan), they wrote:

> The capacity of a nation to use the sea is based upon the character and numbers of its population, the character of its government, the soundness of its economy, the quality and numbers of its harbors, the extent of its coastline . . . and the location of homeland, bases, and colonies with respect to sea traffic. . . . A warring nation that has achieved a predominant capacity to use the sea is said to have command or control of the sea [which] consists of (1) the ability to defend one's own sea communications and (2) the ability to deny the enemy the sea communications he requires to carry on the war. . . . Bases are indispensable to naval operations for both logistic and strategic reasons . . . needed to replenish, repair and protect fleets and also to maintain them near important communications routes.

They also incorporated naval aviation into sea power theory: aircraft carriers replacing battleships as the most important platforms; the need for fleet concentration reduced; the risk of fleet concentration increased; and "gunboat diplomacy" promoted to "carrier diplomacy" to influence friends, foes, and crises.

Writing during the Cold War, Potter and Nimitz were also more mindful than Mahan of the value of allies in creating and using sea power, whether for basing or supplementing the U.S. Navy. NATO became the first peacetime broad-based naval (and military) alliance, and the United States both supported and relied on the naval capabilities of (once rivals) Britain and Germany, as well as others. Another historical adversary of the United States, Japan, also became an ally and naval partner, though of limited capabilities and reach. Maritime security became collaborative. To this end, U.S. leadership was

---

21 Potter and Nimitz, 1960. This is the standard textbook for generations of midshipmen at the U.S. Naval Academy.

as important as U.S. supremacy, though the latter obviously facilitated the former. Unlike Imperial Germany and Imperial Japan, the United States "multilateralized" sea power. At the same time, American strategy then and now requires U.S. naval power—and U.S. military power in general—to be robust enough to assure national security regardless of the strength and reliability of allies.

With the help of its allies, U.S. sea power went essentially unchallenged during the Cold War, giving the United States the ability to assure maritime security, reinforce NATO, strike the Soviet homeland, and take on a new submarine-based strategic nuclear mission. Although the Soviets invested heavily in naval and long-range, land-based anti-naval capabilities, they were never able to threaten U.S. sea control, much less rival it. With East-West confrontation concentrated on the western and eastern edges of the Eurasian land mass, the Cold War could be described geo-politically as one between a great land power and a great sea power. If the Soviet Union ruled Mackinder's "Heartland" and most of his "World Island," American command of the seas, trade, economy, and defense of the sea-connected "Free World" validated Mahan's thinking. Owing to its sea power, the geographic remoteness of the United States from key theaters of East-West confrontation proved to be more advantageous than disadvantageous. The Cold War also reinforced U.S. reliance on global force projection, much of it by sea and supported by the ability to strike from the sea.

In addition to its limited ice-free, risk-free access to open oceans noted earlier, the Soviet Union's failure, despite considerable effort, to exercise serious sea power in the North Atlantic or Western Pacific suggests a deficit of understanding, commitment, and competence to do so. The Soviet Union had negligible sea-borne trade, being isolated from the Western economy and reliant mainly on commerce with its client states, which with the exception of Cuba were land neighbors. Its main reason to build a fleet was self-protection in the event of World War III, both by holding U.S. naval strike power at a safe distance and by impeding U.S. reinforcement of NATO.[22] This narrow motivation proved inadequate to make the Soviet superpower a sea power

[22] Swartz, 2011, p. 7.

as well. Being a non-trading land power with a military dominated by generals, the Soviet Union lacked the commitment that made Britain, Germany, the United States, and Japan sea powers. It proved the rule that national consciousness of the importance of the seas is needed to provide the resources, patience, and persistence for navies.[23] The only parts of sea power the Soviet Union possessed—ships—are of limited value absent the whole package.

As important as ships are the skills needed to crew and command them. Referring to the officers of the Royal Navy during the 19th century, Robert Massie wrote, "Going from ship to ship as they progressed in age and rank, experienced the sea and learned to command. The ultimate lesson was constant: in the British Navy it was not the ships but the men who won."[24] The same can be said for German, American, and Japanese officers and sailors—and French, Spanish, Dutch, and Portuguese ones before them. Superior British seamanship and confidence on the high seas, whether in the English Channel or off China, were products of generations of experience, which has no substitute.

Operating globally is qualitatively more demanding than operating coastally or regionally. It is also more potent because it gives the global sea power options the regional sea power does not have, such as "swinging" fleets from region to region or surging them from home bases in response to need. Both the Germans and the Japanese erred in calculating that the worldwide span of British and U.S. sea power, respectively, would be a disadvantage against regional sea power; for both Great Britain and the United States were able to bring far forces to bear when required to do so. What can distinguish the best navies from all others is the regularity with which they steam at great dis-

---

23 The Soviets did, however, succeed in placing a significant fraction of their strategic nuclear forces at sea—more specifically, under the sea on ballistic-missile submarines. Although they did not match U.S. prowess in submarine-based strategic deterrent forces (preferring to depend more heavily on land-based missiles), they were able to avoid large-scale detection by U.S. anti-submarine warfare systems. In this regard, substantial U.S. and growing Chinese reliance on submarines for strategic deterrence is not called into question by current technological developments, and will be left outside the scope of this study of sea power.

24 Massie, 1991, p. 374.

tance, detached from their support. When coupled with two-ocean access, as the United States has, such ranges facilitate coverage of high seas, trade routes, and critical waters worldwide.

A land power can be a sea power, as the American and German cases show. But the strategic culture of the land power may relegate its naval service to junior status and fail to attract and develop the personnel required for blue-water superiority. The Soviet Navy never matched its investment in ships with an investment in sailors. In current parlance, the Soviet Union concentrated on the "hardware" of sea power while neglecting the "software." Whether China can master both sides of sea power is a key question to which we will return.

These intangible qualities and the experience it takes to hone them explain why it can take decades to achieve sea control, let alone dominance, even with the industrial capacity for large-scale naval construction. Japan made a national commitment to become a sea power 60 years before Pearl Harbor, and 25 years before crushing the Russian fleet in 1905. Even with extraordinary political and industrial drive, it took Germany 30 years to confront the Royal Navy (at Jutland), and then it fell short. As rising sea powers mount such massive efforts, established ones can invest and maneuver to meet the challenge, as Britain did toward Germany and as the United States did toward Japan and may now do toward China.

The chapters that follow will investigate how Mahan's propositions are withstanding technological and geo-political change, particularly the military-information revolution and globalization. But it seems that his basic explanation of sea power—answering vital national needs, enabling national greatness, reflecting national character, requiring national commitment—is valid still. As we will see, the degree of national commitment is bound to affect the prospect or at least the timing of sea-power competition between the United States and China: The Americans are at a very different point in a very long national learning curve. At the same time, in sharp contrast to the Soviet Union, China depends vitally on sea access and thus has a strong incentive. At present, that access depends on the forbearance of the U.S. sea power, which the Chinese are disinclined to assume.

We will return to the relationship of Chinese and U.S. sea power in the next chapter, after devoting the remainder of this one to the search for relevant lessons from three historical cases, two of them involving the United States and one of them set in the Western Pacific.

Anglo-American Naval Relations

While the United States was in the process of gaining continental size and control, Great Britain was establishing sea power in its fullest sense: a far-flung empire, control of the high seas, the ability to defeat invasion, and unmatched global influence. Following a reduction in ship levels in the wake of the Napoleonic wars and War of 1812, Britain steadily built and maintained a fleet of incomparable scale and strength. The Royal Navy had to fight few pitched battles against rival powers at sea during the rest of the 19th century, prompting Mahan to observe that a state with superior offensive naval capability should not have to use it. Britain's sea power gave it worldwide freedom of action and access, accepting no regional power's sphere of influence. As Spain lost most of its American colonies, British presence in the Western Hemisphere became the largest exception to the Monroe Doctrine.

Relations between the United States and Great Britain were strained for much of the 19th century. Chronic American Anglophobia got a violent boost in the War of 1812 and flared up nearly to the point of hostilities during the Civil War, as London pondered recognition of the Confederacy (which it then declined once it became clear that the Union would prevail).[25] Although the United States frowned on British presence in the Western Hemisphere throughout the 19th century, challenging the sea power that backed that presence was out of the question, especially with more important continental tasks.[26] There

---

[25] When two Confederate emissaries were removed by the U.S. Navy from a Royal Navy ship, outrage in both America and Britain nearly brought on hostilities. Engulfed in a Civil War and being totally overmatched at sea, the United States backed down.

[26] The other persistent, if unrealistic, U.S. strategic notion in the 19th century was to conquer Canada.

was modest American interest in sea power after the War of 1812, but this soon dissipated. Until the very end of the century, the U.S. Navy paled in comparison to the Royal Navy. As late as 1880, Britain outnumbered the United States in major combatants by ten to one (377 to 39).[27] What the Americans lacked in naval tonnage they lacked even more in experience. The formative experience for Mahan's generation of naval officers was the blockade of the Confederacy.

Simply put, the United States lacked the motivation to be a sea power until the late 19th century. Given its expanding size and bountiful natural resources, its economy depended little on foreign trade and therefore little on assured maritime access. U.S. trade in 1845 was essentially at the same level as it was in 1825, roughly one half of which was with Great Britain during this period. Then, Southern cotton trade with British textile manufacturing took off, accounting for most of a doubling of U.S. exports between 1845 and 1860. But this did not impel the United States to invest in a powerful fleet; rather, it made blockade and coastal shelling its most important missions. Although Americans saw British sea power as potentially threatening to their shores and ships, the lack of strong economic interests left the United States without a strategic justification for building a grand, costly fleet. Indeed, beyond its littoral waters, U.S. maritime security was largely afforded by the navy of its would-be rival, Great Britain. Given higher priorities than overseas trade and sea power, America defaulted to the Royal Navy.

The Civil War forced the federal government to build a large (700-vessel) fleet to strangle and bombard the South. In the course of that conflict, the U.S. Navy successfully denied British trade with the South, though London never tasked the Royal Navy with full-scale breaking of the Union blockade. By 1865, the United States had the world's second-strongest navy. However, its purpose was to regain continental control, not to extend power or protect trade globally. Consequently, American naval power contracted dramatically after the Civil War—again, the United States was looking inward. By 1880, although the United States was becoming one of the world's great eco-

---

[27] Naval History and Heritage Command, 2011.

nomic powers, its navy was no better than 12th in strength.[28] This was the U.S. Navy in which Mahan served until he turned to the task of explaining its utter inadequacy.

Meanwhile, the Royal Navy was gradually being transformed from the world's supreme wooden-hulled, sail-propelled force to its supreme steel-hulled, steam-propelled force. While the United States continued to chafe against British defiance of the Monroe Doctrine, enabled by the Royal Navy, it was not until it set its sights on becoming an imperial power toward the end of the century that rivalry with Great Britain affected American thinking about sea power. Given certain parallels between the United States at the end of the 19th century and China at the beginning of the 20th—both being rising powers with expanding interests facing established sea powers—the national mind-set that led a thriving American land power to decide to become a great sea power is worth close analysis. Economics supplied some of the motivation: U.S. foreign trade tripled between 1865 and 1880 (much as China's foreign trade has multiplied in the last quarter-century). But the primary impulse was to be a global power, and the primary obstacle was Great Britain. Mahan identified the way, Lodge furnished the ideology, and Roosevelt supplied the cheer.

Because Mahan presided over the Naval War College in Newport, Rhode Island, his ideas were circulating throughout the U.S. Navy's senior ranks, especially its newest captains and admirals. While American naval officers did not then (and do not now) command such political power that they can claim national resources for naval accounts—as did British, German, and Japanese admirals—they were active in developing modern capabilities. Naval attachés fanned out abroad to glean ideas from more experienced navies.[29] They often encountered German and Japanese counterparts engaged in similar activities. (The Chinese are not the first to "borrow" militarily useful technology from others nations.) As a result, when the United States got around to becoming a sea power, it went directly to steel, steam, long-range guns, battleships, and long-legged cruisers.

---

28 Swartz, 2011, p. 11.

29 Swartz, 2011, p. 11.

A wave of American Anglophobia crested over the Venezuela boundary-dispute crisis (1895), when Roosevelt and Lodge urged war.[30] The *New York Times* front page reported: "Country Is Aroused, Want To Fight England."[31] However, the American hawks' agenda got way ahead of the investment in sea power they needed to carry it out. The U.S. Navy had three battleships to the Royal Navy's 50, against which American ports were defenseless. As it became apparent that the small and untested U.S. fleet would not last long against Britain's naval preponderance—a discrepancy that would take decades to correct—American imperialists shifted their attention to a more inviting target: Spain, a fading power, clinging to its remaining significant possession in the American Hemisphere, Cuba. From this point on, the United States no longer treated Great Britain as a threat to its strategic interests or as a sea power to be challenged.

Just as the United States chose not to take on the dominant sea power—Spain being a softer target by far—Britain chose not to treat the rise of U.S. sea power as a challenge. Turning its attention to more pressing threats, especially the gathering danger of hegemonic war in Europe, Britain stopped sneering at the Monroe Doctrine. Just as London was about to dispatch an armada to the Caribbean to settle the Venezuelan dispute on Britain's terms, Germany threatened to go to war with Great Britain over South Africa. The British then executed a "pivot" of their own: "Within a week America was seen as a potential ally, a fellow English-speaking nation against German imperial ambitions."[32] At the same moment it dawned on the Americans that they would need a massive investment in sea power to end British encroachment in the Western Hemisphere, Germany "frightened England into America's arms," according to Henry Adams.[33]

The British were also realistic enough to see that the United States had the wherewithal to create an unchallengeable sphere of influence

---

[30] The issue had little intrinsic importance but took on inordinate symbolic importance in American politics.

[31] Thomas, 2010, p. 68.

[32] Thomas, 2010, p. 99.

[33] Henry Adams, quoted in Thomas, 2010, p. 100.

in its hemisphere. Moreover, the United States and Great Britain were increasingly interdependent economically, though bilateral trade was more important to the United States than to Great Britain. In 1880, 42 percent of U.S. trade was with Great Britain. By 1895, despite rapid growth in total U.S. trade, its trade with Great Britain was still 38 percent. In the Anglo-American case—though not in others, as we will see—shared interest in maritime security sapped the argument for maritime rivalry. Having diverged for most of American history, U.S. and British strategic interests were increasingly convergent. From America's point of view and Britain's, Anglo-American sea-power rivalry was over before it really began. Confrontation was averted mutually: The United States knew it was not strong enough, *yet*, to challenge British sea power in the Americas; and Great Britain knew that it could not contain the rise of U.S. sea power without exposing itself to the graver risk of German sea power.

Meanwhile, Roosevelt sought war with Spain with his inimitable exuberance. Apart from the merits of liberating the Cuban people, he had two motivations (three, if one counts his burning desire to lead men into battle): a conviction that a foreign war was needed to unify and invigorate the American spirit, and a justification for the construction of a world-class navy.[34] Roosevelt got what he wanted: a lopsided war with Spain, several American overseas possessions, and a sustained increase in the size and capabilities of U.S. Navy. The event that christened the United States as a sea power and Pacific power was the destruction of the Spanish fleet in Manila harbor by Admiral Dewey's Asiatic Squadron on May 1, 1898. There was celebration not only in America but also in Great Britain, literally. Although naval expenditures climbed from 7 percent to 20 percent of the entire U.S. federal budget from 1890 to 1905, the British were not disturbed. After all, the United States was not challenging British sea power: Germany was.

The "Great Rapprochement" (1895–1914) between the established and rising Anglo-Saxon powers resolved their naval rivalry, not because the United States was dissuaded from becoming a global sea power

---

[34] Roosevelt relished the opportunity to lead troops into battle, having experienced danger and excitement only in hunting game. Thomas, 2010.

but because British and American interests were compatible and, with the rise of Germany, increasingly convergent. When the United States got bogged down in a nasty counterinsurgency campaign against a Filipino resistance movement following the Spanish-American War, its eagerness for empire and thus its need for naval strength receded.[35] Still, by the time of the Great White Fleet's global circumnavigation in 1907–1908, the U.S. Navy had 22 battleships, 25 cruisers, and a total of 180 warships. While the Royal Navy, twice that size, still had global superiority over the U.S. Navy, it chose not to compete in the Western Hemisphere, given other and more critical regions and challengers, e.g., Germany and potentially Japan.

Even as Great Britain turned its main attention to Germany, the United States treated the Royal Navy as at least the benchmark, and perhaps the potential rival, of U.S. sea power. In 1912, Woodrow Wilson's Assistant Secretary of the Navy—Franklin D. Roosevelt, following in his cousin's footsteps—exhorted Congress "to buy and build dreadnoughts until our Navy is comparable to any other in the world"—by clear implication, Great Britain's. He argued that the American sea control must "extend all over the Western Hemisphere . . . a thousand miles into the sea . . . and wherever our commerce may be."[36] By the outbreak of World War I, the United States had replaced Great Britain as the supreme sea power in the entire Western Hemisphere, and the British were not prepared to contest this. The American digging of the Panama Canal, following aborted European attempts to do so, was both inspired by and a factor in the pursuit of this supremacy.

Two features of early American sea power bear noting in relation to Mahanian thinking. First, U.S. motivations, thus capabilities and operations, passed through stages: territorial defense, i.e., preventing British or Spanish bombardment (neither of which was much of

---

[35] Evan Thomas, in *The War Lovers* (2010), suggests that Roosevelt in particular was less enthralled with expansionism than he was with war and the chance to lead troops. Having become famous by leading his Rough Riders up "San Juan Hill," Roosevelt largely ceased to become an advocate of conquest and empire, right through his presidency.

[36] Franklin D. Roosevelt, quoted in Walter R. Borneman, *The Admirals: Nimitz, Halsey, Leahy, and King—the Five-Star Admirals Who Won the War at Sea*, New York: Little, Brown and Company, 2012, pp. 75–76.

actual threat); coastal patrol, i.e., securing littoral waters for approaching and departing shipping; economic security, i.e., preventing attack on merchant ships, convoys, commercial activities, and assets wherever required (e.g., in China); support for expeditionary operations (e.g., in Cuba and the Philippines); and global power-projection. For a prolonged period (roughly 1895–1930), the Americans looked to sea power to achieve regional control but *not* to challenge or deny rivals in other regions. Loosely speaking, Japan and Germany followed the same sequence (as China may be doing now).

A second notable feature of early U.S. sea power is that its operations, reflecting its staged development, were distinctly *non*-Mahanian. As late as the 1920s, U.S. naval forces were "divided into numerous separate 'force packages' . . . in order to more effectively carry out their principal missions: troop and cargo transport, convoy protection, anti-submarine and anti-surface-raider warfare, and blockade."[37] Not until war with Japan did the U.S. Navy conform to Mahan's model of the functionally consolidated and physically concentrated battle fleet—and then, of course, centered on the aircraft carrier at least as much as the battleship.

By the end of the century of its supremacy, Great Britain could no longer meet the standard of dominating *all* of its potential sea-power rivals: rapidly industrializing and outward-looking Germany, the United States, and Japan. It was forced, in effect, to cede the Western Hemisphere to the United States and then to ally with the United States and Japan against Germany, its most immediate threat (and later with the United States against Japan).[38] The United States took advantage of British worldwide commitments and demands to become the leading sea power in its region. (As we will see, this is a pattern Germany tried to exploit at the time and China might try to exploit, vis-à-vis the United States, today.)

Beyond naval strength, it was clear by the end of the 19th century that the economic and industrial potential of the United States would soon surpass Britain's. As the world's strongest economy and first to

---

37 Swartz, 2011, p. 11.

38 Swartz, 2011, p. 10.

industrialize, the British knew well that sheer industrial scale could decide sea power competition between two states both committed, all else being equal. Although lacking comparable naval experience, so strong was the United States becoming, and so concerned were the British with Germany's rise, that the Crown launched a pro-American propaganda campaign at this time in hopes of winning an invaluable ally for the Great War to come. In essence, the established sea power did not challenge the rising one; and while the Americans considered the Royal Navy the standard against which to measure theirs, they had no compelling economic or security reason to contest it.[39] Once Americans' ingrained Anglophobia faded, both states recognized that their interests were increasingly aligned.

It is impossible to say whether British and American naval accommodation would have occurred but for London's growing anxiety about Germany and its naval ambitions. There were other pressures and constraints acting on His Majesty's Government at that time, not least of which was economic belt-tightening that necessitated making strategic compromises.[40] In any case, the Anglo-American case suggests that two great sea powers—one established, one rising—operating in the same waters are not inevitably on a course to competition, much less confrontation. It must also be said, though, that while the Royal Navy continued to operate throughout the Western Hemisphere, it did not challenge U.S. sea control; indeed, it *could not* do so because of demands elsewhere. As the U.S. Navy grew, Anglo-American maritime rivalry was not merely defused but even transformed into a century of maritime alliance against common adversaries.

While this is encouraging for the Sino-U.S. case, it is important to remember that the United States explicitly claimed and Great Britain reluctantly accepted an American hemisphere of influence. Britain recognized that the United States would surpass it in the economic and

---

[39] Interestingly, the United States brought on the Spanish-American war less for economic reasons—American corporate leaders were at first opposed to war—than for humanitarian ones. The ability of Hearst's Yellow Press to whip up war fever was based largely on his journalists' descriptions of Spanish atrocities. Thomas, 2010.

[40] First Sea Lord Sir John "Jacky" Fisher is reputed to have said at the time: "We're out of money, so we'll have to think."

industrial wherewithal to maintain world-class sea power—something the United States does not recognize in China today.

Anglo-German Naval Competition and Conflict

In contrast to Anglo-American naval competition, which was resolved peacefully and turned into maritime cooperation, Anglo-German naval competition helped drive a friendly relationship into violent conflict, including at sea. Again, Great Britain was the textbook sea power (quite literally in Mahan's texts). Its grand strategy was to dominate the seas in order to prevent invasion, assure access to its empire, and, if need be, deny access to would-be enemies. Sea power enabled Britain to keep Europe's continental struggles at arm's length, with the option to intervene with small expeditionary forces to restore the balance of power, as it did against France and would against Germany.[41] As a requirement of this strategy, London was determined to maintain naval forces at least as capable as any pair of adversaries that might combine against it.

Britain's policy of sea dominance confronted the growing interest of newly formed, outward-looking Germany in assured maritime access. Like the United States and Japan at the time (and China at present), Germany was rapidly becoming an industrial power. Its production of steel doubled every decade from 1870 to 1900, surpassing Britain's production in the 1890s.[42] Its rail system grew from 3,500 miles in 1850 to 26,000 miles in 1900. Just as Great Britain's dependence on foreign trade grew as it industrialized, so did Germany's. As of 1914, the British and German Empires transacted 40 percent of world trade (27 percent British and 13 percent German).[43] For both, the lion's share

---

41 British strategy was to weigh in and, if need be, intervene with small expeditionary forces on the weaker side of any European conflict. This strategy was found to be inadequate when His Majesty's government had to intervene on a massive scale to prevent German hegemony on the European continent.

42 Chris Butler, "The Spread of Industrialization Beyond Britain (c. 1850–1900)," 2007.

43 Edgar Crammond, "The Economic Relations of the British and German Empires," *Journal of the Royal Statistical Society*, Vol. 77, No. 8, July 1914.

of that trade was sea-borne. The two owned 53 percent of world merchant shipping.[44] With industrialization and the need for materials and markets, German trade grew very rapidly, doubling total exports and imports from 1897 to 1907.[45]

As Germany industrialized, it had a growing requirement for raw materials and markets reachable only by sea. It also sought to make up for its late start as a colonial power by obtaining overseas possessions both for their economic potential and for prestige. Yet Germany's access to colonies, resources, and markets was at the pleasure of the Royal Navy, the supremacy of which Great Britain was determined to preserve. British strategy was therefore viewed in Berlin as threatening to Germany's economic health, imperial control, and standing as a great power. So Germany embarked on a campaign not just to become a sea power but to break Britain's sea supremacy, which the British would regard as a major threat to their interests and strategy. It took Germany about 25 years, starting around 1880, to become capable of testing British supremacy. During that time, Anglo-German relations soured and turned hostile. Although their naval competition did not cause World War I, it gave the British a reason to suspect Germany of hegemonic intentions and to fear German power. Consistent with British policy of aligning against whichever power threatened Europe's balance, Britain moved toward alliance with its traditional enemy, France. In turn, this meant that Germany and Britain would be on opposing sides when war occurred.[46]

Germany's commitment to sea power was the product of backroom lobbying by a navy that was dwarfed in political influence by a German—largely Prussian—army that had won successive wars and enabled Bismarck to create the country. Admiral Tirpitz and his col-

---

[44] Crammond, 1914.

[45] Crammond, 1914.

[46] The immediate British casus belli was German violation of Belgian sovereignty and neutrality, once Germany was felt compelled by the developments of August 1914 to attack France preemptively. But in the 20-year course of events leading to that point, the transformation of Anglo-German relations from amity to enmity was in part the result of the distrust sown by naval rivalry.

leagues managed to convince the instinctively Anglophile Kaiser that Great Britain was Germany's enemy, determined to deny it access to the high seas and the essential resources and new colonies beyond them.[47] The admirals, taking a page from Mahan, framed the problem not as *naval* special pleading but as a *national* imperative: Failure to back a sea-power strategy would have grave consequences for a nation that was becoming vitally dependent on sea-borne trade. The challenge was also expressed in terms of fairness and pride: What entitled Britain to deny Germany access to the seas and the possessions, resources, and markets beyond them that Britain itself enjoyed? As German wealth, power, and patriotism grew, so did German resentment of a British policy that meant to keep Germany not only down but under Britain's control. This sentiment meant that German sea power would have political support and therefore generous resources—one of Mahan's criteria for success.

Once German naval officers bent their (pliable) civilian masters to the view that Britain was an enemy, the prophecy would be fulfilled—the British, feeling threatened, began to behave that way. The admirals and their political allies were not subtle about their target or their objective. The Second Naval Law (1890), authorizing construction of a High Seas Fleet, began with the following:

> To protect Germany's sea trade and colonies . . . there is only one means: Germany must have a battle fleet so strong that even for the adversary with the greatest sea power [Great Britain], a war against it would imperil [the British] position in the world. For this purpose, it is not absolutely necessary that the German battle fleet should be as strong as that of the greatest naval Power because a great naval Power will not, as a rule, be in a position to concentrate all its striking forces against us. But even if it should succeed in meeting us with considerable superiority . . . the defeat of a strong German fleet would so substantially weaken the enemy that its own position in the world would no longer be secured by an adequate fleet.[48]

---

[47] Massie, 1991.

[48] Massie, 1991, pp. 180–182.

This formulation was known as Tirpitz's "Risk Theory." German strategy anticipated that Britain would find it increasingly difficult to safeguard its global interests and meet challenges from multiple rising sea powers. Matching British sea power was not a necessity, since the British could not concentrate their forces on the High Seas Fleet the way the Germans could concentrate theirs on the Royal Navy. Indeed, once the Imperial High Seas Fleet was built, Britain would be hesitant to confront it and thereby endanger its "position in the world." At that point, Germany would have the sea control it required.

Late-19th-century Germany had the means as well as the will to become a great sea power. In addition to its rapidly growing economic capacity and industrial prowess, Germany would overtake Britain as world leader in science and technology. From 1871 to 1914, it had more Nobel Prizes in Science than Britain, France, Russia, and the United States combined.[49] As it applied technology to naval capabilities, Germany's ships were second to none in quality, speed, and weaponry. Exploiting the benefits of a late start, Germany was not encumbered with a large fleet of wood-hulled sailing combatants. In contrast, Great Britain was slow to shift to iron, steel, and steam. In addition, the German navy developed seamanship and leadership with uncommon speed. The 20 years it took Germany to become a sea power was quick by historical standards.

Britain's response to Germany's expanding continental and sea power was to recommit to naval supremacy. Although Great Britain was slow to grasp the significance of Germany's new-found sea power commitment (despite the Germans being so explicit about it), once it did it threw itself into construction of bigger, swifter, and better-armed capital ships, including *Dreadnought*-class battleships and fast, light "all-big-gun" cruisers. The British certainly understood that Germany would become a formidable sea-power rival once it put its mind and means to it. For the British, an all-out naval construction race would be a major challenge with a great cost and an uncertain outcome, especially with global requirements and other sea powers looming.

---

[49] Massie, 1991.

In fact, the Germans' Risk Theory—that undermining British confidence in a crisis did not require that Germany match Britain's navy—nearly worked. In the years leading up to World War I, Britain shifted to a "one-power standard," articulated in 1912 by First Sea Lord Winston Churchill as 60 percent superiority over Germany. Thus, the German challenge forced the British to accept significant risk in other regions (e.g., the Pacific) in order to frustrate a rising sea power in the region of their greatest interest. But the Germans brought this British response on themselves by explicitly threatening Britain's ability to deny them access to the high seas.

This begs the question of why Great Britain insisted on having the ability to deny Germany the sea access it demanded and genuinely needed. Why did Britain not offer Germany essentially the same space it offered the United States to become a sea power? Anglo-German relations were friendlier prior to their naval rivalry than Anglo-American relations were for most of the 19th century. In fact, Great Britain and Germany had common, historical adversaries: France and Russia. Anglo-American kinship was no closer than that between the British and German crowns, related by blood. Against this backdrop, the British could have offered Germany some sort of joint maritime security. They did not. While British statesmen might have moved in this direction, British admirals surely would have opposed it.[50] After all, a policy of retaining sea supremacy justified a major modernization of the large but aging Royal Navy. Both the British and German admiralties were politically assertive, and neither regarded competitive naval construction as entirely unwelcome.

If anything might have pushed Great Britain to steer away from competition and confrontation with German sea power, it would have been economics, not statesmanship. Fearful of German capacity and determination, feeling the growing burden of the shipbuilding race, and hoping to shift resources to social programs, Britain's Liberal government did propose a mutual slowdown in warship construction (1908–1909). But the Kaiser and his admirals would have no part of

---

50 Admiral John "Jacky" Fisher consistently opposed any restrictions on British sea power. Massie, 1991, p. 431.

an arrangement that would have codified Britain's numerical advantage. According to Albert Ballin, an influential German shipping magnate alarmed by the turn in Anglo-German relations, "Tirpitz . . . did not wish to negotiate. He wanted no settlement. He wanted only to build ships." The British admiralty was only slightly less enthused about an Anglo-German deal to limit construction. The initiative was rejected by Berlin and dropped by London.[51] In any case, limiting ship construction would have been, at best, a patch on the expanding gulf between British and German sea-power objectives.

The story of the Anglo-German naval arms race prior to World War I—told by Robert Massie in his brilliant book *Dreadnought*—was like the Soviet-American nuclear arms race during the Cold War (except that the latter did not end in hot war). Strategists, military leaders, and politicians in both capitals seized upon intelligence and news of the latest ship designs and building plans of the other to expand and upgrade their own naval capabilities beyond any requirements except those of the competition's internal logic. The established power was not entirely reactive to the moves of the rising one. The British were the first to lay the keels of new classes of more powerful ships, leap-frogging German designs and forcing Berlin to follow suit. If this dynamic was fed by suspicion, it created even more suspicion.

While the Royal Navy remained larger and operationally superior right up to World War I, Germany was closing the gap. In 1898, when Germany's effort went into high gear, the Royal Navy had 329 warships compared with 68 for Germany. Ten years later, Germany had added 162 warships, while Great Britain had added only 8. The British, as noted, were modernizing while the Germans had to expand and modernize. If the Germans forced a quantitative naval arms race, the British set the pace for a qualitative one. Naval technology was such that each rival was building a mirror image of the other, with a particular emphasis on the offensive power of the concentrated battle fleet (just as Mahan had prescribed).

Broadly speaking, although the established sea power was the first to industrialize and the rising one had only just become a uni-

[51] Massie, 1991, pp. 792–800.

fied state, the two were roughly equivalent in capacity to support sea power. While Germany had greater economic and industrial potential, it also had major land interests that Great Britain did not. Being evenly matched, neither had cause to back off for lack of confidence in its ability to compete. The British had strong reasons not to abandon their strategy of maintaining sea control by maintaining supremacy. The Germans had equally strong reasons to pursue relentlessly their goal of breaking the ability of Great Britain to deny access—or, according to the Risk Theory, to make prohibitive the expected costs to the British of threatening Germany's interests and navy.

It is important to reiterate that the Germans took *direct* aim at the Royal Navy, figuratively in building the High Seas Fleet and literally in their plans to break British sea denial. As we will see also in the Japanese-U.S. case (and might also witness in today's Sino-U.S. case), there is no better way to justify and focus the pursuit of sea power than to place that of a rival and potential enemy squarely in the crosshairs. Yet, this approach can be counterproductive and even dangerous insofar as it provokes the targeted, established power to invest even more in its naval capabilities, to design them specifically to defeat the rising power, to view that power as an enemy, and to draw up war plans to defeat it.

It is impossible to say how the events of 1914 would have unfolded had the collision between Britain's sea-power standard and Germany's sea-power ambition not occurred. Again, the war was precipitated by events and alignments separate from the naval arms race. Yet, the role of Anglo-German sea-power rivalry in the lead-up to war should not be underestimated. The German naval challenge precipitated not merely a British in-kind response but also a change in British foreign policy—the abandonment of "Splendid Isolation" from the Continent's disputes and alignments in favor of weighing in the side of the powers opposing the increasingly powerful Germany. Even as German admirals depicted British sea power as evidence of hostile intentions toward Germany, British statesmen saw the growing German High Seas as a leading indicator of a strategic if not existential threat. "[A]s Britain began to fear the German Fleet, it feared also that the greatest military power in Europe would not aspire to become a great naval power unless it wanted to dominate the world. . . ."[52]

As a consequence, in Massie's words,

> Britain became . . . a partner of its erstwhile enemies, France and Russia. The alienation of Britain from Germany and its growing partnership between Britain and France and Britain and Russia, were caused by fear of the German Fleet. "It closed the ranks of the Entente," said Winston Churchill. "With every rivet that von Tirpitz drove into his ships of war, he united British opinion . . . the hammers that clanged at Kiel and Wilhemshaven were forging the coalition of nations by which Germany was to be resisted and finally overthrown."[53]

The title of Mahan's monumental work, *The Influence of Sea Power upon History*, is no exaggeration in the case of Anglo-German naval competition.

It is not unreasonable to suggest that the race itself and the animosity it fueled could have been avoided if British and German statesmen had been energized by the idea that two nations had largely shared interests when it came to trade, freedom of the seas, and even the possibilities of maritime cooperation. But this is a very big *if.* The British were not prepared to accept and cooperate with Germany's growing naval might any more than the Germans were prepared to trust the British to use their navy to safeguard the seas for German use. Just as Great Britain was unwilling to accept a German sphere of influence in Europe, Germany was unwilling to accept British control of the high seas. Moreover, statesmen in London and Berlin did not have the political "chops" to overrule naval interests; indeed, they had largely bought into the argument that sea power was a national imperative—economic and strategic—not a naval demand. (Because such "what-if" and "missed-opportunity" analysis illuminates choices faced today by the United States and China in the Western Pacific, we will return to it.)

---

[52] Massie, 1991, p. xxv.

[53] Msssie, 1991, p. xxv.

An epilogue to the story of Anglo-German naval rivalry and conflict is pertinent to our study. Having failed to neutralize Britain's sea-power advantage, and having lost World War I, Germany of the Third Reich chose not to invest heavily in a surface fleet in the run-up to and during World War II.[54] Instead, it concentrated on a strong submarine force to threaten British and American naval forces and to cripple the shipping that the allies relied on for reinforcement. The Germans considered anti-naval capabilities more promising, more cost-effective, and more essential than those of a powerful surface fleet. It is interesting to speculate whether a Nazi aircraft-carrier force on the American or Japanese scale would have affected the war in Europe and the Atlantic. Strategically, Hitler and his strategists were captivated not by the idea of becoming a sea power, perhaps in league with Japan, but rather by the need for "living space" to Germany's East—in the "Heartland" that Mackinder argued was the key to command of the "World Island" and ultimately the World.

While Nazi Germany appreciated the importance of the seas, especially to its enemies, it opted for sea-denial capabilities by exploiting submarine technology rather than imitating the Anglo-Saxon fleets (as Imperial Germany had done). With the advance of technology, sea power was no longer defined by battle fleets or confined to clashes of battle fleets. The Battle of the Atlantic—which Churchill called the "dominating factor of the war" on which "everything happening elsewhere depended"—pitted allied bombers against German U-boats that eluded surface escorts to attack convoys with war supplies.[55] Sea power had evolved from power *upon* the sea to power *of* the sea. Although the technology of his day did not require Mahan to make the distinction, he would surely have been comfortable with it.

Hitler and his lieutenants never read *The Influence of Sea Power upon History*, as far as we know. Had they, they would have found

---

[54] Nazi Germany had a small but capable fleet of surface combatants, which was not used until the invasion of Norway, and then only after some pressure by the German admiralty. During the Cold War, the Federal Republic continued Germany's tradition of naval excellence and was NATO's ally in the North Atlantic.

[55] Quoted in Borneman, *The Admirals*, 2012, p. 276.

an alternative to the theory that controlling Eastern Europe was the key to controlling the world. They might also have understood why defeating two sea powers would be harder than conquering continental neighbors.

Japan and the United States

Germans may not have studied Mahan between the Wars, but we know that the Japanese did so all along. Although Mahan wrote the sea-power script for his own country, the Japanese followed it exactly. After emerging from self-isolation in the mid-19th century, Japan became a sea power and as a result a great power: a seafaring island; the first non-Western country to industrialize; determined to produce more than it consumed; increasingly dependent on foreign trade; growing stronger economically and technologically; capable of unified national purpose and commitment; relentless. The irony, of course, is that it was the United States that pierced Japanese insulation, resulting in a Japanese commitment to sea power that eventually was turned against the United States. Fifty years from the time Commodore Perry opened Japan, it had arrived as a world-class sea power by its spectacular and surprising destruction of the Tsar's fleet at the Strait of Tsushima during the Russo-Japanese war (1905), where both Japanese ships and Japanese seamanship excelled.

Like the United States, Japan graduated its navy in phases from coastal defense to trade-route security to regional sea power. Japanese sea power continued to increase in size, quality, and experience until capable of forcibly challenging the United States for control of the Pacific in World War II. However, the United States—unlike Great Britain in the Western Hemisphere—was not about to acquiesce in foreign hegemony in the Western Pacific, euphemistically called the Greater East Asian Co-Prosperity Sphere by the Japanese. This contradiction between Japanese and American sea-power purposes set the stage for the collision to come, prompting the obvious question about parallels with China and the United States today.

Although allies during World War I, the Japanese saw the United States and Great Britain as their rivals and prospective adversaries in the Pacific. Even in victory, Britain emerged exhausted from World War I. Although the British had built more ships than it lost during the war, political commitment and resources flagged after 1919, when British defense expenditures as a whole were "cut to the bone."[56] Though it had not suffered losses comparable to the European powers, the United States came through wary about global responsibilities and ambivalent about sea power. A post-war fleet-expansion plan died on the floor of Congress. The United States did, however, send much of its fleet through the Panama Canal to form the Pacific Fleet in 1920.

While influential Americans continued to favor sea power in the aftermath of World War I—President Wilson, an internationalist, called the navy "our natural bulwarks"—this sentiment was swamped by isolationism. Ironically, it was one of the original advocates of American globalism and sea power, Lodge, who engineered the Senate's refusal to ratify U.S. membership in the League of Nations. The economic argument for internationalism and naval strength was erased by Depression and protectionism. U.S. foreign trade peaked in 1920, was flat until 1929, and then plummeted. With Theodore Roosevelt gone and Mahan's books gathering dust, the U.S. pursuit of sea power went into reverse. Apart from interest in the aircraft carrier, contraction of the U.S. Navy in size and strength continued in the 1920s and accelerated with the onset of the Depression. Both the need and ability to pay for a powerful navy declined: By 1933, U.S. foreign trade was one-third what it was four years earlier.[57]

Hoping to preserve their advantages and avert renewed naval competition, Great Britain and the United States organized an arms control conference that concluded in 1923 with an agreement to restrict naval capabilities, with those of the United States at the same level as Britain's and those of Japan at 60 percent: the so-called 5:5:3 formula.

---

[56] British naval and military spending cuts following World War I were justified by an assessment that the country faced no enemy and expected at least a decade of peace ("The Ten Year Rule"). Potter and Nimitz, 1960, p. 477.

[57] U.S. Census Bureau, 2012.

Ambivalent toward sea power, the United States was comfortable with these limits—though, mindful of aviation's promise, it negotiated an exemption to permit two new aircraft carriers to be built. While Japan's government agreed, its admirals never accepted the limits because of their belief that Japan needed a navy no less than 70 percent of the total size of the U.S. Navy if it were to prevail in a war in the Pacific. Japan renounced its obligations under the treaty in 1934, at the nadir in American sea power.[58]

Unscathed by World War I, Japan was poised to exploit the reduction of British and American sea power in the Pacific, owing to fatigue and isolationism, respectively. From 31 warships in 1898, the Imperial Navy grew to 230 by 1908. By the time its aggression was in full swing in the 1930s, Japan had the strongest navy in the Pacific in numbers and quality. In 1940, its surface fleet had grown to 375, all in the Pacific. Like the Americans, the Japanese were committed to aircraft carriers, adding 18 from 1940 to 1944.[59]

For Japan, sea power permitted conquest, which in turn demanded more sea power, which in turn enabled an economic system that provided the resources for naval expansion. While imperial and militaristic urges were factors in Japan's quest for both sea power and conquest, economics was the main driver—or, more precisely, the readiness to use force to make and protect economic gains. Japanese foreign trade grew rapidly from 1891 to 1914 (from $110 million to $600 million), then exponentially after World War I. From 1931 to 1937, despite the Depression, Japanese total trade tripled. Japan was clear of the Depression by 1933 and sustained an average annual growth of 5 percent during the 1930s. Economic growth was mainly in manufacturing, especially heavy manufacturing. Japan required more ore, more fuel, and more markets, all of them overseas.

At the time their rivalry heated up, Japan and the United States were not especially interdependent economically. U.S. direct invest-

---

[58] Seventy percent would suffice because Japan has a one-ocean requirement, whereas the United States has a two-ocean requirement.

[59] The United States Strategic Bombing Survey, *The Effects of Strategic Bombing on Japan's War Economy*, Appendix Table C-150, December 1946.

ment in Japan (and elsewhere) declined sharply after 1930. Japan's trade with the United States, which had grown from 12 percent of its total trade on the eve of World War I to 45 percent in 1927, plummeted during the Depression. Total U.S. trade contracted from $9.5 billion in 1929 to $2.9 billion in 1932. Thanks to the Smoot-Hawley Tariff Act of 1930, U.S. imports fell by 68 percent during those years. U.S. trade with Japan was only 7 percent ($400 million) of total U.S. trade in 1929 and 6 percent ($120 million) by 1934. As Japan's non-U.S. trade rapidly grew, it shifted to East Asia in the 1930s, exploiting the difficulty of depressed Western powers to supply their Asian colonies. Its export push, including yen devaluation, in the 1930s was targeted toward Asia. Japan needed to export textiles and other products in order to satisfy a growing need for far more strategic imports, not only to sustain economic growth but also to prepare for the war it was expecting.

Japan's drive for resources led to the accumulation of naval might and the conquest of territory, the most ambitious of which was the annexation of Manchuria in 1936. Then Japan's production-propelled economy stalled, owing to declining external demand, and accelerating militarization of the economy caused a trade deficit because of the need for war-making materials. Total Japanese trade in 1929 was 4.2 billion yen, declined by 1932 to 2.8 billion yen, but then expanded to 6.8 billion yen by 1938. It also shifted markedly from the United States to East Asia.

In sum: U.S. foreign trade declined sharply during the 1930s; Japanese trade grew during that same period; U.S.-Japanese trade became insignificant for both; and Japanese trade became increasingly dominated by demand for resources to support militarization and war preparations. One can infer from this that the United States was becoming less dependent on the security of oceanic trade routes; that Japan was becoming more dependent on them; and that there was little Japanese-American economic interdependence that might have restrained their behavior toward one another.

These striking economic trends provided the context in which the Japanese became increasingly anxious about a resurgence of U.S. interest in sea power, oriented especially toward the Pacific. It was another

Roosevelt who had previously served as Assistant Secretary of the Navy, Franklin Delano, who dusted off the ideas of Mahan midway into the Depression. Fundamentally a job-creation and industrial-rescue measure, the National Industrial Recovery Act of 1933 authorized new construction of cruisers and other combatants. This was followed by significant expansion, with particular stress on aircraft carriers. By 1940, the United States had 15 battleships, 6 aircraft carriers, and 478 ships in all (over three times the number in 1933).[60] From then on, U.S. naval power grew rapidly while U.S. foreign trade idled.

Apart from domestic economic recovery, the motivation behind the renewed U.S. commitment to sea power in the 1930s was Japan's growing navy and aggressive conduct in East Asia. By the time of its abrogation of the Washington Naval Treaty, Japan was acting on its imperial ambitions, in part to subdue China and in part to secure access to the raw materials of Southeast Asia. In addition to increasing naval construction from the mid-1930s on, the United States redeployed much of its Pacific fleet from California to Hawaii to dissuade Japan from further expansionism. Japan interpreted this as U.S. intent to challenge the Imperial Navy, to establish both sea control and sea denial in the Western Pacific, to threaten Japan's increasingly vital sea lines of communications, to starve Japan of strategic materials, and to thwart Japan's national strategy. While the United States did not directly threaten Japan's access to fuels and other materials until just before World War II, the Japanese were not being paranoid in reading U.S. sea power as directed squarely at them. When negotiations failed, the Japanese felt compelled to attack the U.S. fleet at Pearl Harbor.

If Germany and Great Britain clashed over sea power despite largely compatible national interests, Japan and the United States did so because their interests were in conflict. Competition in building and deploying aircraft carriers did not poison Japanese-American relations the way competition in building and deploying dreadnoughts had poisoned Anglo-German relations. Rather, it was Japanese aggression in a region of great importance to the United States that aroused U.S. concern and led Roosevelt and his admirals—King, Leahy, Halsey,

---

[60] Naval History and Heritage Command, 2011.

and Nimitz—to meet this challenge head-on. The United States was surprised tactically on December 7, 1941, but not strategically. It christened five new aircraft carriers in the six years prior to Pearl Harbor, all of which fought against the Japanese fleet.[61]

Despite Japan's impressive ship-building capability during World War II—until U.S. strategic bombing destroyed the yards—its fleet was mostly destroyed by superior U.S. naval forces, built by an even more impressive U.S. naval construction program. By 1945, the U.S. Navy was the largest and strongest the world had ever known.[62] Notwithstanding its extraordinary economic, industrial, and technological development from 1850 on, Japan was overmatched by the United States in all means to compete in sea power. Japan's GDP per capita was 29 percent of the United States' in 1929 and, despite the more severe U.S. Depression, still only 38 percent in 1940. The rising power could have known that war with the established power, fought largely at sea, would go badly if the latter maintained its will and marshaled its resources. Japan's leaders were badly mistaken to expect that Pearl Harbor and subsequent U.S. reverses would cause American will to buckle. Of course, it had precisely the opposite effect. U.S. Chief of Naval Operations Ernest King vowed to avenge Pearl Harbor by the "destruction of Japan as a sea power, regardless of how long and how much treasure it takes."[63]

Moreover, Tokyo felt that it had no choice but war, and that the best chance for success was to destroy the U.S. fleet at the outset. Indeed, Japan's top admiral was disappointed that the attack on Pearl Harbor had destroyed some aging battleships and other combatants but had inflicted no damage on U.S. carriers, submarines, or shipyards. Japanese realization that U.S. naval-strike and naval-construction capabilities would eventually overwhelm Japanese sea power led to another daring Japanese offensive six months after Pearl Harbor: The Battle of Midway resulted in the loss of all four of the carriers Japan had used

---

[61] USS *Ranger* (CV-4), USS *Yorktown* (CV-5), USS *Enterprise* (CV-6), USS *Wasp* (CV-7), and USS *Hornet* (CV-8).

[62] Swartz in Saunders et al., 2011, p. 12.

[63] Quoted in Borneman, *The Admirals*, 2012, p. 211.

to attack Pearl Harbor—marking the beginning of the end of Japanese sea power and the beginning of the American dominance in the Pacific that exists to this day.[64]

The imbalance in American and Japanese capacity for sea power contrasts with the rough equivalence in that respect between Great Britain and Germany during their rivalry before World War I. The British thought they could maintain naval superiority, and the Germans thought they could present the British with unacceptable costs if the Royal Navy had to take on the High Seas Fleet. In the Anglo-American case of 1880–1895, although the British enjoyed a huge advantage over the Americans, it was already apparent that the United States was on a trajectory of growth and industrialization that would eventually overwhelm Britain's ability to compete, especially in a region of much greater importance to the United States. As a consequence, the superior established power yielded, in effect, to the rising one in order to deal with a graver threat elsewhere. Arguably, only Japan grossly overestimated its ability to compete.

Lessons from Theory and History[65]

Mahan's ideas were the product of his times: They presumed that great powers would be rivals, they reflected Britain's success, and they sought

---

64 Borneman, *The Admirals*, 2012, p. 260ff.

65 Readers may be interested in lessons from another analysis of rising sea powers (Swartz in Saunders et al., 2011). In summary:

1. Rising sea powers are a feature of rising political, military, and economic powers.
2. When a rising economic and political power decides to build a formidable navy, it usually can do so.
3. A country has to be rich and smart to be a rising sea power.
4. All rising sea powers have eventually collided with other naval powers in combat—sometimes with other rising powers and sometimes with powers that had achieved supremacy.
5. When a rising power builds a strong navy, other strong powers strengthen their own navies.
6. Technological superiority matters in the short run, but in the long run naval technology flows more or less freely across borders among the world's most powerful nations.

to ignite American interest in sea power. Nor was Mahan infallible: His insistence that the concentrated surface fleet's offensive power was the core of sea power followed from temporary technological limits—the close ranges of communications, sensors, and weapons. Conceptually, he failed to see the powerful logic and unfortunate effects of spiraling naval competition, the Anglo-German rivalry having barely begun. It is not clear that Mahan would have become the geo-strategic celebrity he did had Lodge and Roosevelt not discovered him and run with his ideas. Still, Mahan's work—especially in its synthesis of economics, geography, and international power-politics—remains a useful frame of reference, and in any case has had enduring influence with sea-power strategists the world over.

As Mahan explained, nations with both dependence on sea-borne trade *and* substantial economic, industrial, and technological means will seek sea power: Great Britain, Imperial Germany, the United States, and Imperial Japan all fit Mahan's model; indeed, they read his script. Those with sufficient means but insufficient incentive—the Soviet Union, for instance—will lack the national consciousness, consensus, culture, and commitment it takes to become true sea powers. While a prerequisite for economic success, sea power also can enlarge such success and thus augment the capacity for still greater sea power. In particular, Great Britain and Japan—neither one a land power with abundant natural resources—built "outsized" naval capabilities in order to gain economic strength and in turn support such capabilities.

When a sea power sets its requirements as a function of the actual and projected capabilities of another sea power, the results may include costly competition in naval investment, an accumulation of forces otherwise unjustifiable, growing distrust and animosity in general, and dangerous proximity at sea. This dynamic occurred in the Anglo-German and Japanese-American cases, but less so in the Anglo-American case. When one power's determination to have assured access (sea control)

7. Rising powers and their navies may earn the respect and friendship of others.
8. All formerly rising sea powers except for the United States have eventually become declining powers. Most of the navies of formerly rising powers are eventually allied with the United States.

threatens or is seen as threatening another power (sea denial), competition is especially fierce. Again, this is how the Germans and Japanese read British and American intentions, respectively, and not without reason. While Japan and the United States had incompatible interests, owing to U.S. refusal to accept Japan's aggression and regional hegemony, Great Britain and Germany had fairly convergent interests when their sea-power rivalry began. That rivalry contributed to the deterioration of Anglo-German relations and led to a realignment of European powers that turned a Balkan crisis into a world war.

While economics—dependence on resources, markets, and thus secure trade—motivate pursuit of sea power, so does the ambition to be and be recognized as a great power, to gain world influence, and to acquire possessions or clients. The accumulation of colonies and clients with valuable resources adds further to the requirement for maritime security and sea power. While Great Britain, Germany, and Japan were more acquisitive colonial powers than the United States, American sea power contributed greatly to the winning of allies and clients in the 20th century.

Becoming a full-fledged sea power takes a generation or more. Not only does it take that long to build a great fleet, but also a fleet cannot be great without naval experience and excellence. The United States and Germany were the quickest to assemble sea power in numbers and quality. Both embraced the latest and best technology (whereas the British were encumbered with a legacy fleet and slow to change). The United States and Germany were rapidly becoming world-class industrial-technological giants, and both had made clear strategic decisions to achieve sea power expeditiously. In any case, it does not necessarily take a generation to challenge an adversary's sea power if there is a way to do so without imitating it. Though it had no Mahan-style fleet, Nazi Germany might have won the Battle of the Atlantic had long-range allied bombers not reasserted Anglo-American sea control. Since Mahan's time, technology has made sea power a highly asymmetric endeavor, with under-sea, over-sea, and land-based capabilities all part of the equation.

In the case of Great Britain and the United States, the established sea power did not deny the rising one, competitively or operationally. Instead, the two, though unfriendly for most of the 19th century, came to rely on each other for maritime security. When an established sea power accommodates a rising one, rivalry may give way to maritime spheres of influence or cooperation. Had Great Britain signaled receptivity to Anglo-German cooperative maritime security, it might have undercut the argument of Admiral Tirpitz that it was Germany's enemy. The United States could have made no such offer to Japan because Japanese aggression made cooperation impossible and U.S. sea-denial necessary.

Economic interdependence does not prevent sea-power competition, but the absence of interdependence can weaken inhibitions. U.S. trade with Great Britain made up the largest share of U.S. trade and was important to U.S. economic growth. Germany and Great Britain were somewhat interdependent, though obviously not enough to avoid an arms race and war. Japanese-American trade had plummeted in the 1930s and was negligible by the time rivalry in the Pacific was in full swing.

Politically, strong "naval interests"—uniformed, industrial, and political—make conditions more favorable for competition than cooperation. Generally speaking, with both budgets and fleets expanding, British, German, American, and Japanese governments were under little pressure to cooperate. Although Britain's global demands and multiple challengers compelled it to accept the rise of U.S. sea power, entrenched British naval advocates were otherwise committed to a strategy of preponderance. The German admiralty wanted a big navy even if it required turning Britain into an enemy. Japanese factions that favored challenging the United States and Great Britain in the Pacific were largely unopposed. Roosevelt and other political and opinion leaders were determined to achieve independent American sea power; indeed, the U.S. Navy itself has never been an especially powerful political force compared with its Imperial Japanese, German, and British counterparts.

Table 1 assesses the main factors affecting sea-power rivalry in these cases, looking for patterns to help explain outcomes. We will apply this analysis to the Sino-American case after considering U.S. and Chinese interests and strategies, technological developments, and prospects for cooperative maritime security. For now, some preliminary observations are worth making.

First, all cases bear on the Sino-American case in that established and rising sea powers alike possessed economic, technological, and industrial power, relied heavily on sea-borne trade, and sought global status and influence.

Table 1
Assessment of Historical Cases of Sea Power Rivalry

	Great Britain and the United States	Great Britain and Imperial Germany	The United States and Imperial Japan
Reliance on sea-borne trade	Great Britain: High United States: Medium (and growing)	Great Britain: High Imperial Germany: Medium (and growing)	United States: Medium Imperial Japan: High
Bilateral economic interdependence	High	Medium	Low
Relative economic and industrial capacity and potential	Great Britain: High United States: High (and growing)	Great Britain: High Imperial Germany: High (and growing)	United States: High Imperial Japan: Medium
Naval technology, skill, and experience	Great Britain: High United States: Medium (and growing)	Great Britain: High Imperial Germany: Medium (and growing)	United States: High Imperial Japan: High
Conflicting national interests, including contested spheres of influence	Low	Medium	High
Potential for cooperative maritime security	High	Medium	Low
Political influence of naval interests	Great Britain: High United States: High	Great Britain: High Imperial Germany: High	United States: Medium Imperial Japan: High
Outcome	Accommodation, cooperation, alliance	Contributed to antagonism and likelihood of war	Primary cause and instruments of war

Second, the Anglo-American case differs from the Sino-American case in that Great Britain was not prepared to sustain a challenge to the Monroe Doctrine. This left the two with compatible global interests, increasingly friendly relations, and a path to cooperative maritime security. In contrast, an exclusive Chinese sphere of influence in East Asia is incompatible with U.S. economic and security interests, although China will in any case have some influence upon its neighbors as much by virtue of its commercial as its military importance.

Third, the Japanese-American case differs from the Sino-American case in that the established power was actively and explicitly threatening sea denial to counter the rising power's aggression in East Asia. Japan considered this to be a direct threat to its interests and goals (however ignoble). Moreover, the two had little economic interdependence, and Japan had no prospect of matching U.S. economic-technological-industrial capacity as applied to sea power.

Fourth and finally, the Anglo-German case is particularly interesting for the Sino-American case: As described above, Great Britain and Imperial Germany had divergent interests in Europe but mostly compatible interests beyond Europe, including in secure trade. The two were economically highly interdependent. Great Britain had been the 19th century's top commercial, financial, technological, and industrial power, but Germany was closing the gap. Great Britain was unmatched as a sea power; Germany was expanding from a continental power to a sea power as well.

The Anglo-German sea-power rivalry is a cautionary tale. Despite a shared need for secure trade and access to colonies and raw materials, there was no attempt to cooperate in meeting this need. Rather, each power treated the other's naval build-up as directed at it: The Germans saw sea denial as the British intent, and the British saw the Germans as a challenge to their imperative of sea control—and both were essentially right in their perception. This led to a frenzied arms race, increasingly muscular capabilities (not otherwise needed), deepening suspicion, antagonism, and preparations for a war that would bleed the vitality and power of both countries—a path neither Americans nor the Chinese want to follow.

This raises an obvious question: Whether, and how, might the Anglo-German case have ended amicably? Put differently, might the logic of cooperation in pursuit of shared interests have prevailed over the logic of power politics? Might Great Britain and Germany have disproven Mahan's fresh theory that sea power was inherently competitive?

As already explained, admirals and sympathetic politicians in both Great Britain and Imperial Germany saw no alternative—or chose to see no alternative—to rivalry. Had these "naval interests" been less sure of themselves or less influential, Germany might not have been so explicit and blatant in challenging British sea power, and Great Britain might have suggested a path to mutual maritime security. But such *statesmanship* was not prominent, nor even present, in either London or Berlin. Alternatively, objective and realistic calculations in either capital might have moderated the conceit there and perhaps in the other capital. Of course, rationality and humility—like statesmanship—were in short supply in pre–World War I Europe.

Nonetheless, as a thought experiment, it is worth following the Anglo-German case down the path untaken. This invites two further questions: What proposal for collaborative maritime security *might* the British have made to the Germans, consistent with Britain's core interests? Why *might* the Germans have responded favorably, consistent with German interests? The answers could shed some light on whether and how, a century later, it might be possible for American and Chinese sea power to co-exist peacefully, consistent with the interests of both, in the Western Pacific.

Had British political leaders recognized that Germany was determined and perhaps entitled to have assured access to and passage through the high seas, they would have known that trying to maintain sea denial would inevitably stiffen German resolve and end in confrontation. At a minimum, they might have offered some sort of non-denial pledge covering Germany's peaceful use of the seas. Even if no more than a promise, such a declaratory policy could have weakened the claim of the German admirals that Britain meant Germany harm—the claim the Kaiser bought. The British might have reinforced this by proposing regular exchanges, joint exercises, and joint patrols between the two navies, under the watchful eye of statesmen. Of course, such an approach would likely have been resisted by the British admiralty, which was increasingly suspicious of Germany and also held much of British political elite in its thrall. With British supremacy under pressure on several fronts—emerging American and Japanese power, demoralizing conflict in South Africa, a rising power in Europe—London was clinging to its core advantage: dominant sea power. The failure then (and lesson for today?) was in the failure of political leadership.

Had Great Britain followed such a course, German leaders, starting with the Kaiser—though not much of a statesman himself—would have at least been in a quandary. The German admirals, being interested above all in building a powerful fleet, would have argued that British capabilities, not stated intentions, should determine not only German capabilities but also German policy. But with other challenges the new Germany faced on the Continent, a reasonable alternative to a costly naval arms race with Great Britain might have been intriguing. With hindsight's benefit, it is clear that cooperating rather than competing with British sea power would have served German interests. Had the two navies, despite their own misgivings, then pursued maritime security cooperatively, the good faith and trust of the two states—friends until lately—might have been preserved. In any case, German leaders should have known that for Germany to explicitly depict the Royal Navy as justification for the High Seas Fleet would provoke the expansion and modernization of the Royal Navy.

This what-if excursion is not only counterfactual but hardly plausible. For starters, politics would have worked against it. Again, the British commitment to dominant sea power was not just naval but *national*—just as Mahan theorized. It was accepted by political and commercial elites as the only way for Great Britain to be the world's leading power and excel economically, and it was ingrained by centuries of cumulative success. As important, Britain's ability and willingness, when push came to shove, to deny potential adversaries use of the seas was considered a strategic imperative. For Britain to have assured Germany that it had no reason to fear British sea power would have contradicted British strategy.

In turn, it is doubtful that the Germans would have placed much faith in a British assurance that German sea access would not be denied.

The Kaiser who bought the admirals' logic about British hostility to Germany was unlikely to accept a British pledge of restraint over the objections of those very admirals. With British strategy depending on naval supremacy, a promise to not use that supremacy would not have slowed Germany's dreadnought construction. On top of the counter-strategic quality of cooperative maritime security, strong industrial interests in both countries acquired a stake in the ship-construction race, regardless of its costs and risks.

Thus, given British and German strategic goals and national mind-sets, it is hard to think of a British assurance that would have prevented the costly and ultimately destructive rivalry that ensued. As Massie puts it:

> Why, the Kaiser and millions of his people asked, should England claim to command the sea as a right? At any moment, the British Navy could blockade the German coast, bottle up German ships in harbor, and seize German colonies. Why should the German Empire exist on British sufferance? Why should German greatness come as a gift from another people? Geography dictated confrontation. . . . A German Navy strong enough to protect German merchant shipping . . . and guarantee unimpeded passage to the oceans meant, in the last resort, a German fleet able to defeat the British Navy. . . . This Great Britain would never permit.[66]

It takes little imagination to put the Chinese in German shoes: Why should Chinese access to resources and markets vital to its future exist on American "sufferance"? Why should Chinese greatness come as a "gift" from the United States? Meanwhile, like the British a century ago, Americans today can project that as China acquires the ability to target and strike U.S. sea power in the Western Pacific, the consequence would be that U.S. access to those vital waters would be at Chinese sufferance. To paraphrase Massie, this the United States would never permit.

As it played out, the Anglo-German case is discouraging for those, like the author, who believe that U.S. interests in the world and

---

[66] Massie, 1991, p. xxiv.

East Asia are best served by the peaceful and cooperative development of Sino-U.S. relations. Powerful forces, akin to those of the Anglo-German case, propel China and the United States toward sea-power competition and possible confrontation in the Western Pacific. China wants to be a great power with a regional sphere of influence; it has growing global economic interests and reliance on sea-borne trade. It sees the United States as at least capable of and perhaps intent on sea denial in and beyond the Western Pacific. At present, China depends, by default, on U.S. sea power to provide security for its global trade. But it regards U.S. sea power as threatening in the Western Pacific, and it has rebuffed U.S. initiatives to explore cooperative maritime security.

At the same time, Chinese admirals lack the political clout that Tirpitz and his colleagues had. Nor is American sea power on a domestic-political pedestal the way British sea power was. Because the United States is the world's leading power in virtually *all* respects, sea power does not have inordinate importance as it did in Britain when the Royal Navy was synonymous with greatness. The United States is in a stronger geo-strategic position today than Great Britain was a century ago. Politically, at least, perhaps Washington and Beijing have more latitude than London and Berlin did to pursue cooperation at sea.

Finally, the Anglo-German case suggests that Sino-U.S. economic interdependence will not prevent a naval arms race, suspicion, antagonism, and increased probability of conflict. However, as a preliminary hypothesis, *if* China does not insist on a sphere of influence at the expense of the United States in the Western Pacific, and *if* the two pursue maritime security with mutual restraint or cooperation, *then* confrontation like that between Britain and Germany, not to mention Japan and the United States, is avoidable.

True, this is not the only way to avoid a sea-power clash in the Western Pacific: The United States could yield to China's potential for sea denial. But that could endanger U.S. interests in a region of unsurpassed importance—as implied by this book's title—and so is treated as a path to avoid. So we will need to return to the question of whether and how China and the United States can realize maritime security cooperatively—a "hard sell" in both countries, to be sure—after examining their respective strategies and the impact of technology in the Western Pacific.

CHAPTER THREE

U.S. and Chinese Interests and Sea Power in the Western Pacific

"Even though the leading object of war be defense, defense is best made by offensive action."—A. T. Mahan[1]

Introduction

Whether the United States and China compete, cooperate, or merely co-exist at sea depends on how each sees its national interests and the role of sea power in defending and advancing them. In the light of theory and history, this chapter examines U.S. and Chinese interests and strategy in the Western Pacific. It looks especially at American and Chinese thinking about trade and other maritime interests, about the operational and political purposes of navies, and about sea control and sea denial. Obviously, sea power figures importantly in U.S. strategic thinking, globally and in the Pacific, as it has for a century. Yet it is unclear how this thinking will be affected by the expansion of Chinese power, influence, and aspirations in East Asia. For China's part, though it has just begun to contemplate sea power and is unlikely in any case to follow the path of earlier sea powers, its potential is obvious.

In considering the Sino-American case, two distinctions are worth reiterating: The first is between power *upon* the sea and power *of* the sea—the former being just an aspect of the latter. Sea power in the larger sense can be achieved with capabilities under and over the sea, and also with capabilities from land, in space, and in cyberspace. Mahan theorized that sea power is more than naval power, and

[1] Mahan, *Naval Strategy*, 1911, p. 205.

the impact of technology since his day confirms this. In this regard, anti-naval capabilities, of the sort China is emphasizing, figure importantly in sea power (as allied bombers did in the Battle of the Atlantic). Armed services other than the navies may have a role in sea power: marines, obviously, but also air forces and armies with surface-to-surface missiles.

The second distinction is between sea control and sea denial, the former being the ability to assure access to important waters for naval forces, shipping, and extraction of resources, and the latter being the ability to disrupt such access, even temporarily. As we will see, the United States still has a major stake in sea control in the Western Pacific. The Chinese are fearful of U.S. sea denial, and even more fearful of U.S. capabilities to strike China from the sea. While they probably cannot achieve sea control, they are intent on denying the United States low-risk access to seas off China's shores. Thus, China is pursuing *asymmetric* sea power, but sea power nonetheless.

While many factors affect the purposes and capabilities of both American and Chinese sea power in the Western Pacific, the largest factor is what the *other* country does or is expected to do. True, each has naval missions that are not directly linked to the other: China uses surface combatants to harry vessels of neighboring nations in disputed waters; the U.S. Navy is poised to stop pirates from interfering with shipping in the Strait of Malacca. But the sea-power capabilities of China and the United States are becoming coupled in a similar way as those of Great Britain and Imperial Germany and then the United States and Imperial Japan were, which is hardly encouraging.

In developing new capabilities, the U.S. Navy now treats China as its main "planning case," as the People's Liberation Army (PLA) has treated the United States since at least the mid-1990s. While the two have not become locked in a spiraling naval arms race like the Anglo-German one, the logic of competition is evident in that a move by one triggers a counter-move by the other, and so on. This coupling is especially strong and consequential in relation to China's belief that U.S. naval strike forces in the region are threatening to its security and its interests. China's response has been to improve anti-naval and other A2AD—distinctly anti-U.S.—capabilities as a high priority. The U.S.

response to this Chinese response to U.S. force presence is sure to produce another Chinese response. The new U.S. "Air-Sea Battle" strategy (discussed later) targets the Chinese A2AD capabilities to target U.S. forces. Already, the Chinese are investing in the anti-satellite (ASAT) and cyber-war capabilities that can disable the command, control, communications, computers, intelligence, surveillance, and reconnaissance (C4ISR) on which Air-Sea Battle depends. The United States could, in turn, feel constrained to counter this with ASAT and cyber-war capabilities of its own; maybe with the threat of escalation. As in chess, every move in this game is more strategic and more menacing than the last.

Our horizon for analysis is 20 years. Given how complex and fluid this region and the Sino-U.S. relationship are, to say nothing of technology's blistering pace, predicting that far into the future is more sport than science. But recall that 20 years is roughly the time it took Great Britain and the United States, Great Britain and Germany, and the United States and Japan to settle their naval rivalry—peacefully in one case, violently in the other two. So now is an important moment to consider the dynamics and implications of American and Chinese maritime strategies. Twenty years seems like a long time to avert conflict; yet, once the logic of rivalry locks in the parties, momentum can get stronger with time. At sea, being on a collision course does not make a collision inevitable. But the extended length of time it takes to turn a large ship requires early awareness that one's course may lead to trouble.

The entry point for this analysis is not the dynamics of technology and military capabilities of the United States and China but the economics of production and trade. After all, Mahan's theory of sea power rested on economics: To prosper, nations must produce more than they need; so they must import materials and export products, mainly by sea; so they need sea power to assure access, protect trade routes, and, if need be, sever the access and trade of their rivals and enemies. Because the United States and China are the world's two largest and most productive economies, face political and demographic pressures for growth, are major trading partners, and depend vitally on sea-borne trade, we will start there.

Chinese and U.S. Trade

The United States became a sea power when its economic development caused it to turn to foreign trade over a century ago. China, though much poorer per capita, is starting to become a sea power at essentially the same stage in its development. In both cases, rapid economic growth and industrialization not only fostered trade but also provided resources and technology to build modern naval capabilities. Both the United States and China have benefited from globalization, a salient feature of which has been the expansion of their bilateral trade. The chief effect of this trade has been a dramatic expansion of U.S. imports of products made in China, often with know-how brought there by U.S. firms and financed by the expansion of Chinese credit to the United States. China's ability to sustain rapid economic growth with moderate inflation and America's ability to achieve moderate growth with low inflation and low interest rates depend on this trading and financing relationship. China's dependence on trade in general is all the clearer when considering the need for rapid economic growth to maintain political stability, regime authority, and national cohesion.

Total Chinese trade (exports plus imports) is now approximately $3 trillion (50 percent of GDP), and has been growing at twice the rate of GDP growth (20 percent versus 10 percent per annum) over the past decade. Total U.S. trade is roughly $3.7 trillion (25 percent of GDP), and has also grown at about twice the rate of GDP growth (6 percent to 3 percent per annum). Again, both countries depend predominantly on sea-borne trade, though a greater share of Chinese trade than U.S. trade is sea-borne—about 95 percent compared to 85 percent—because Canada and Mexico are huge American trading partners. Thus, sea-borne trade accounts for about 45 percent of Chinese GDP and about 20 percent of U.S. GDP. By implication, China depends more than the United States does on the certainty that its sea-borne trade is secure, though the United States has far greater naval capability to secure trade than China.

While the United States has more Western Hemispheric trade than China, China has more Asiatic trade than the United States. But both trade extensively with all parts of the world—petroleum from the

Middle East and Africa to both China and the United States, natural gas from Central Asia to China, industrial and commercial trade with Europe for both China and the United States, commodities from Latin America to both, and food-stuffs to China from the United States and elsewhere.

Sino-U.S. trade has more than tripled in the past decade, from about $150 billion to $500 billion, as has the U.S. trade deficit with China, from about $100 billion in 2002 to $300 billion in 2011. U.S. exports to China are consistently less than one-third of Chinese exports to the United States. This deficit is to a large extent financed by Chinese credit: China has accumulated $1.3 trillion of U.S. Treasury securities, making it the U.S. government's largest sovereign creditor.[2] In the past decade, U.S. trade with China has gone from 7 percent to 14 percent of total U.S. trade, while Chinese trade with the United States has gone from 22 percent to 15 percent of China's total trade. Thus, both depend equivalently (in proportion to GDP) on trade with the other, but China's dependence on U.S. trade has declined relatively, even as the total has increased. Still Chinese exports to the United States have grown from about $100 billion to $400 billion per annum in the past ten years (in comparison to growth in U.S. exports to China from $20 billion to $100 billion per annum in the same period). Chinese exports to the United States are about 7 percent of Chinese GDP, and Chinese imports from the United States are 2 percent of Chinese GDP. In contrast, U.S. exports to China are less than 1 percent of U.S. GDP, whereas U.S. imports from China are about 3 percent of U.S. GDP.

Chinese exports to the United States have played and will keep playing a crucial role in the development of Chinese manufacturing, which has been the locomotive of China's growth. On the other hand, U.S. imports from, not exports to, China constitute the most important U.S. interest in trade with China: American consumers, producers, and service-providers alike have come to depend critically on competitively priced Chinese goods—for everything from filling retail-chain shelves to supplying components for complex information systems to providing such systems. Take away Chinese exports and credit to the

[2] U.S. Department of Treasury data.

United States, and both economies would suffer: China from higher unemployment and the United States from higher prices and interest rates.

The Chinese and American economies have become highly interdependent in other ways. China helps finance the U.S. fiscal deficit, enabling politically popular federal spending without raising taxes. Although Chinese imports from the United States are much smaller in volume than U.S. imports from China, Chinese producers have benefited hugely—as American shareholders have profited hugely—from the transfer of technology, management skills, and distribution access that U.S. direct investment has brought China.

In addition, Chinese enterprises are now deploying capital accumulated in large part from trade with the United States to invest directly in international production.[3] China's increased ownership abroad should increase its stake in a healthy global economic system and, as a corollary, maritime security. In this new phase, the United States looks increasingly to growing demand in China to make up for sluggish growth at home and in Europe and Japan. That the United States counted heavily on Chinese growth to lead it and the rest of the world out of the contraction of 2008–2009 suggests how much Sino-American economic interdependence has grown. Chinese collaboration will become more critical in managing global economic institutions and policies.

Sino-U.S. economic interdependence, using bilateral trade as an indicator, is substantial but declining in proportion to total trade, especially for China. Still, it is hard to imagine how the two economies, or the entire global economy, would weather a collapse of their economic relationship. Indeed, that specter may be the best guarantee that the two will avoid conflict, over sea power or anything else. Contrast Sino-American interdependence with the relatively small amount of U.S. trade with and investment in Japan prior to World War II, which declined sharply during the 1930s. (The similarity between Sino-American trade at present and Anglo-German trade prior to World

---

[3] *The Economist*, "Being Eaten by the Dragon; Chinese Takeovers," November 13, 2010, p. 81.

War I will be taken up later.) Insofar as U.S. economic interests in East Asia warrant continued U.S. ability to preserve stability and influence in the region, it is clear that those interests are bound up in maintaining conditions that permit Sino-American economic ties to flourish. The United States remains a power in the Western Pacific not only because China is a potential danger but also because China is an economic partner.

At the same time, China's dependence on sea-borne trade—nearly half its economy—is feeding Chinese anxiety about the security of that trade. Chinese writings on sea power show heightened awareness of the yawning discrepancy between the importance of China's sea-borne trade and the inadequacy of China's sea power. Recall similar concerns in late-19th-century Germany, also industrializing and beginning to look outward. The security of China's expanding trade, and thus of its economic growth, currently depends on American sea power, globally and regionally. This is not unlike the reliance of the United States on the Royal Navy to safeguard its trade, before becoming a sea power itself at the end of the 19th century. Given that the United States then decided, in essence, that it could count only on itself to secure the trade that fueled its growth, China's interest in sea power should come as no surprise to Americans. Strategically, if ironically, the United States is disinclined to allow the Chinese the measure of sea control in East Asian waters that it insisted on in the Western Hemispheric waters a century ago.

In theory, the mutual economic interest of China and the United States in sea-borne trade, a lot of it with each other, suggests the possibility of a cooperative approach to maritime security. However, three Chinese concerns militate against maritime cooperation with the United States: First, China needs the ability to back its maritime claims and to protect its own trade, at least in its region; second, U.S. sea power is a putative threat to China's trade; third, U.S. sea power is a putative threat to China itself. Notwithstanding Sino-U.S. economic interdependence and shared interest in maritime security, the dependence of China's economy on sea-borne trade may, on balance, argue for sea-power rivalry, not cooperation, with the United States in the

Western Pacific. This impulse would cause China to try to end U.S. sea control while expanding its own sea control in the region.

The logic of confrontational sea power, consistent with how Mahan expected powers to behave, fits with China's interest in reducing the ability of the United States to threaten China and frustrate its wider regional interests and ambitions. The same basic logic explains why the United States is not about to cede to China the responsibility to secure the trade and control the seas of East Asia. In sum, in analyzing U.S. and Chinese interests and strategies in the region and beyond, we have to start by admitting that economics are as likely to excite as to temper sea-power rivalry.

U.S. Interests[4]

U.S. interests in East Asia reflect the region's burgeoning economic strength, its growing demands for global resources, and the influence of its strong states on world politics. East Asia's economy has become the engine of world growth: Over the past decade, the developing economies of Asia have grown at an average of 8.5 percent per annum, while the major developed economies (including the United States, the European Union, and Japan) have grown at an average of 1.3 percent per annum—a pattern that is forecast to continue for at least another five years.[5] East Asia's human capital is vast in number, surging in productivity, and benefiting, if unevenly, from political reform. Its hunger for minerals, thirst for oil, and impact on the environment all have global consequences. Asian powers—China (increasingly), Japan (still), and India (prospectively)—have worldwide interests and roles. Conflict in the region, especially if it involves these powers, could endanger global security and prosperity.

In addition to risks of East Asian instability, the region's importance demands that the United States prevent it from becoming a Chi-

4 This discussion of U.S. interests in East Asia draws heavily on unpublished RAND research led by James Dobbins and co-authored by the author.

5 International Monetary Fund World Economic Outlook Databases, June 2011.

nese "sphere of influence." Because this consideration figures heavily in U.S. strategy and U.S. sea power, the term bears further definition. Like it or not, as East Asia's largest country by far, as a budding world power, and with an outward-oriented economy, China is bound to have a huge role in East Asia. Not only is the United States unable to prevent this, its own stake in China's success argues against trying—thus repeated American assurances that it will not try to contain China. A peaceful, stable, prosperous region that is under Chinese influence but entirely accessible to the United States might not be injurious to U.S. interests. In that case, the United States could learn to live with China leading in East Asia in most dimensions of power: conventional military, economic, diplomatic, demographic, and culture. Such conditions need not exclude the United States, weaken its economy, threaten its security, or preclude Sino-U.S. cooperation.

A much more objectionable version of a Chinese East Asian sphere of influence would be one in which China could claim and exercise the prerogatives of power: bullying its neighbors; "resolving" disputes on its terms unilaterally; dictating foreign policies of other states (e.g., in regard to Taiwan); weakening bonds between the United States and its regional friends; harassing U.S. military forces or restricting their freedom of action; and erecting regional economic arrangements disadvantageous to the United States, e.g., closed trade zones—in a word, hegemony. In classical balance-of-power and sea-power theory, this is the behavior implied by sphere of influence. After all, it was how great powers played their great, "zero-sum" games. From time to time, even the United States exhibited some such conduct in its hemisphere.

Yet, with economic integration, sturdy institutions, agreed norms, and belief in "positive-sum" outcomes, perhaps spheres of influence need not exclude and damage powers outside the sphere. By this reasoning, the United States could be more sanguine than it is about China's growing prominence in East Asia. However, the combination of the region's importance, uncertainty about China's behavior as its power grows, and the potential for instability argues against American complacency. Chinese dominance of East Asia *could* come at the expense of critical U.S. interests, if not immediately then in time. The use of force by China to seize disputed territory would have dire consequences for international order and rule of law. That other East Asian states have also brandished force to stake out their maritime counterclaims underlines the region's potential for instability in the event of U.S. disengagement or exclusion.

In any case, the United States cannot ignore that Japan, South Korea, Australia, Philippines, Thailand, Vietnam, Taiwan, and other U.S. friends—important states in their own right—clearly see the waxing of Chinese power and waning of American power and influence as harmful. That the United States has formal defense alliances with several of these only bolsters the need for balancing Chinese power and, if need be, countering its use. For all these reasons, the United States should and likely will oppose a Chinese sphere of influence in East Asia, at least until it becomes clear from China's behavior that there is no need to worry. Put simply, the United States will need to treat East Asia as a great power would unless China does *not*.

Refusal to allow another power to dominate this region, in this sense, has been a constant of America's foreign policy since it became a great power, sea power, and Pacific power a century ago. From the 1930s on, U.S. strategy has been to block hegemonic control of East Asia, even at the cost of war. Conforming to classical balance-of-power theory, it has put its weight on the weaker side: China (versus Japan) during World War II; Japan (versus the Soviet Union) at the outset of the Cold War; China again (versus the Soviet Union) after 1972. U.S. security interests and responsibilities in the region did not decline with the end of the Cold War; if anything, they have increased because of the region's growing importance.

The United States has persistent and potentially rising security concerns in Northeast Asia, where the defense of South Korea and Japan are binding obligations, where nuclear confrontation is possible, and where the fate of North Korea is unclear. Further south, the peaceful resolution of the Taiwan dispute is important to the United States because it is predisposed to intervene militarily if Taiwan is attacked and also because it would have grave strategic and political consequences if democratic Taiwan were to be swallowed by China. In Southeast Asia, U.S. interest declined after the Vietnam War but is on the rise now because of the growing importance of this area's waters and states, most of which now seek U.S. security ties.

Throughout the region, long-standing U.S. defense relationships are being re-invigorated and reshaped by regional concerns about the implications of unchecked Chinese power. The purposes of the U.S. alliance with Japan have gradually expanded beyond the protection of Japan to the protection of joint interests and peace in the region. There is talk of the U.S. Navy returning to Subic Bay, its former base in the Philippines (though not likely on its former scale).[6] The United States also is developing defense cooperation with Vietnam and India, also motivated by mutual concern about the rise of China. While the United States disavows the intention to encircle or align East Asia against China, what the Chinese see is a region in which its allies are few—two, if one counts Burma—poor, isolated, and unreliable, whereas U.S. allies are prospering and growing in number.

Although China does not at present seem to be intent on the conquest or domination of East Asia, it has threatened military force to press its claims in territorial disputes. It insists that Taiwan is part of the People's Republic, and one should assume it would go to war if necessary to prevent the island's independence. China has resorted to low-grade force to back its fishing rights and resource-exploitation rights in the East China and South China Seas. It has also sided with and propped up an increasingly desperate and unpredictable nuclear-armed North Korean regime, much to the alarm of South Korea and Japan.

Regional jitters due to Chinese military power have been aggravated by unease over U.S. steadfastness, especially during the wars in Iraq and Afghanistan. At present, the United States appears resolved to back its East Asian friends, old and new, in the face of Chinese pressures. This is clear from U.S. diplomatic opposition to Chinese attempts to bully states bordering the South China Sea and from U.S. support for South Korea in the face of provocations by North Korea, China's ally. Failure to stand alongside its friends would deplete U.S. influence with these important states and possibly weaken their resolve to resist intimidation. In the case of Japan and South Korea, there is an

---

6 *Jane's Defense Weekly*, article by Michael Cohen, October 11, 2012.

additional risk that faltering U.S. steadfastness would tempt them to acquire nuclear weapons. Overall, owing mainly to China's economic success, the steady expansion and reorientation of its military capabilities toward the Pacific, and signs of its growing reliance on force, East Asia may be entering a period of instability.

Under these conditions, the instinct of the United States—true to its policy since becoming a Pacific power a century ago—is to renew its commitment to regional equilibrium, to its friends (China's neighbors), to the peaceful resolution of disputes, and to the unrestricted use of the international waters by its shipping and naval forces.[7] This is a matter not just of U.S. regional strategy but of U.S. global strategy. In its latest national defense strategy, the U.S. government has made clear that its preoccupation with the Middle East and South Asia since 2001 has been succeeded by the recognition that its global interests demand greater attention to Asia.

East Asia is a region of global importance not only economically but also in addressing international security problems of U.S. concern around the world. Japan, Australia, and South Korea, for example, have to varying degrees supported the United States in stabilizing the Middle East and South Asia and in countering the proliferation of nuclear weapons. Indonesia, the Philippines, and Thailand are important in stemming the spread of violent Islamist extremism. Moreover, equilibrium and peace in East Asia are essential if the United States is to confront threats to itself and its interests elsewhere in the world, as it did in the decade following 9/11. Now, with the United States struggling with mounting debt and domestic challenges—nagging unemployment, lagging education, and sagging infrastructure—East Asia's stability takes on added significance.

East Asia's global importance is the product of decades of unprecedented regional peace and calm, owing to the restraint of its strongest states, including Japan and China, and fostered by U.S. military presence. Conversely, turmoil, aggression, or conflict in the region could not only endanger U.S. interests there but also weaken U.S. ability to

---

[7] The Obama administration's "pivot" is laid out in The White House, *Sustaining U.S. Global Leadership: Priorities for 21st Century Defense*, January 2012.

meet economic and security challenges globally, including at home. Although East Asia has long been free of turmoil, aggression, and conflict, the potential for trouble exists:

- in Northeast Asia, precipitated by the recklessness or collapse of the Democratic People's Republic of Korea
- over Taiwan, if current promising cross-Strait political trends are reversed
- in the East and South China Seas, over territorial-maritime boundaries and resources
- in case of renewed border confrontation between China and Vietnam or India or Russia.

Asia's continued economic vitality and interdependence may inhibit hostilities over these outstanding problems.[8] But there is no guarantee of this: Even if Asian economies continue to prosper and trade, the growing military strength, reach, and assertiveness of China could increase security concerns and the risk of conflict in the region. Note that China figures in all four potential sources of conflict just mentioned, and that in all four the Chinese claim they have important concerns or prerogatives of national defense or sovereignty. Note as well that the potential for regional instability lies mainly in the relationship of an increasingly powerful China with former adversaries: Taiwan, South Korea, Japan, Vietnam, and India. How China uses its increasing power and reach, as well as how these states and the United States respond to China, could determine whether the region stays stable, its economy stays strong, its disputes are resolved peacefully, and key Asian states play constructive roles in tackling global problems.

At the same time, U.S. interests in East Asia also include the rewards of economic cooperation and the prospect of global security cooperation with China itself. Of all Asian nations—arguably all nations worldwide—China has the greatest potential to help or hinder the United States in meeting security challenges, elsewhere and in the region. Solutions to problems of energy security, maritime security, and

---

[8] Observation from James Dobbins of RAND.

climate change depend heavily on Chinese cooperation, which could involve costs to China. So too does the growth of the world economy, the health of the trading system, and the effectiveness of international institutions, such as the United Nations, the World Bank, the International Monetary Fund, and the World Trade Organization. U.S. and Chinese interests beyond East Asia are not always aligned: take their differences over democratic revolutions in the Arab world and over sanctions on Iran, for example.

On the whole, though, U.S. and Chinese outlooks are more convergent outside of than inside East Asia, where the two increasingly elbow for favor. Thus, U.S. interests in Sino-American global cooperation could be affected, for worse or better, by Sino-American relations in East Asia. This is bound to affect how the United States reacts to the growth of China's regional power, including its challenge to American sea power.

In summary, the enduring U.S. interests in and toward Asia are to

- maintain a healthy, integrated, rule-based world economy, for which Asia is vital
- preserve Asian stability notwithstanding the rise of China and the risk of great-power rivalry
- keep Asia free of aggression and conflict, including the settlement of disputes by force
- sustain close relations with traditional and new partners, especially Japan, Korea, and India
- nurture Sino-American partnership in meeting global security and economic challenges.

China is the fulcrum of these U.S. interests. Just as a cooperative China could advance them, a belligerent and unchecked China that spurns international rules could imperil them. Because the United States still plays a vital balancing role in the region, Chinese attempts to diminish that role and expand its own could destabilize the region. Moreover, if American power were to recede as Chinese power grows, China could be more tempted to use force against its weaker neighbors.

At the same time, U.S. resolve to not abandon its role in East Asian security may put it and China on a collision course.

U.S. Strategy Toward China

Because China could be a threat to U.S. interests in a vital region or a valued collaborator on the world stage—or both at once—U.S. strategy toward it is fraught with dilemma. Treating China primarily as a danger to be countered in East Asia could convince Beijing all the more to challenge U.S. power there and to reject partnership on global security matters. Yet, ignoring the risk that China will destabilize East Asia, in hopes of avoiding confrontation there and facilitating cooperation elsewhere, could reward and invite Chinese pressure in the region. Managing the tension between U.S. regional and global interests vis-à-vis China—between countering it on one plane and engaging it on another—is the defining challenge in the design and execution of U.S. China strategy.

Of late, the U.S. response to China's growing regional power has been *de facto* military containment. While U.S. declaratory policy stresses desire for cooperation, countering China has become the principal rationale for the forward American military presence in the Western Pacific. But military presence must conform to a larger strategy. The United States is still feeling its way for the right approach, having had no modern experience with a phenomenon quite like the rise of China. Of other great powers since the United States became one, Great Britain soon became a partner, whereas Imperial Germany, Imperial Japan, the Third Reich, and the Soviet Union were, conveniently, unambiguous enemies.

The last of these is especially unhelpful as analog. Unlike the Soviet Union, China's integration into the global economy, which accounts for its success and strength, makes it impossible to contain economically. The United States and, even more so, its Asian allies depend critically on Chinese trade, investment, and financing. By the same token, China's lack of an expansionist design or ideological mission makes it awkward and perhaps impossible to contain politically: Most states in the region would prefer constructive relations with China. East Asia has no multinational alliance like NATO to make explicit and effective a region-wide alignment against China—though again, China's recent intimidating behavior has caused several of its neighbors to appeal to the United States for security.[9] Although the United States has very capable military allies in the Western Pacific, the two largest—Japan and South Korea—have historically concentrated on national self-defense, leaving the United States to shoulder nearly all responsibility to keep the region stable in the face of China's rise.

Although it does not seek an anti-China alliance, the United States is trying to improve its regional defense posture vis-à-vis China: updating its defense relationships with traditional allies, deepening security cooperation with India and Vietnam, and concentrating more forces on Guam, which is becoming a hub—temporarily less vulnerable—for U.S. power projection to and throughout the region. Most recently, the U.S. government has declared that it will "pivot" its geo-strategic emphasis from countering Islamist extremism in the Middle East and South Asia to ensuring East Asian stability in the face of China's rise. Of course, the Chinese read these measures as directed against their rightful interests, their quest for regional preeminence, and their territorial security.

U.S. efforts to shore up allied confidence and respond to improvements in Chinese military power and reach could have a dual effect: dissuading the Chinese from threatening or using force, owing to fear of conflict with the United States; yet persuading the Chinese that the United States is intent on keeping down, dictating to, and possibly threatening China. This duality of effects is the result of China's mirror image of the U.S. dilemma: being careful to avoid conflict with the United States, lest China make an enemy of the world's leading power and jeopardize all its economic gains; yet being assertive in claiming the status and deference commensurate with those same gains. (More

---

[9] This uncoordinated but conspicuous regional reaction has resulted from concerns about Chinese actions in the East and South China Seas and its support of North Korea following its sinking of a South Korean naval vessel; the reaction is evident in South Korea, Japan, Vietnam and other Southeast Asian states, and of course Australia.

on Chinese perspectives later in this chapter.) If upgrading of its force posture in East Asia can help the United States restrain the use of Chinese military power there, it can also harden the resolve of the Chinese to improve their military power in order to counter U.S. moves, gain more freedom of action, and lessen the threat to China itself.[10]

As we will see, China has no higher military priority than increasing its ability to neutralize U.S. power, including sea power, in the Western Pacific. Already, the U.S. military is concerned that its operational effectiveness could be reduced and the costs and risks of military intervention increased by Chinese A2AD capabilities. In addition, as PLA ground forces become better equipped and trained, the prospect of fighting a land war with China, near China, looks more forbidding than ever for the United States.[11] As a consequence, the sort of "forward defense" on which the United States has relied in the Western Pacific for 60 years may not be sustainable for long.

Such forward defense—the Seventh Fleet, Air Force bases, Marine Corps and Army forces—has been the hallmark of U.S. commitment to its allies and the region's stability. Yet, continued reliance on that familiar presence, comforting as it may feel to allies, will place U.S. forces at greater risk. This leaves the United States with a vexing choice: reduce its military presence or accept greater risk to U.S. forces that allies find reassuring. This raises an obvious question: How long will allies be reassured by the presence of increasingly vulnerable forces? Unless the United States reworks its military strategy and posture in East Asia, it could end up leaving both its forces and its allies more exposed, and perhaps more tempting targets should China turn aggres-

---

[10] The notion that increasing U.S. military strength could dissuade China from increasing its military strength—in fashion a decade or so ago in some American circles—has proved flat wrong (not to say naïve), in that China has instead increased military spending and focused mainly on countering U.S. power.

[11] In addition to the advantages of geographic proximity, the land forces China could mobilize are vastly greater than those the United States could mobilize. Each year, roughly 10 million Chinese come of military age. Although this number will decline as a consequence of China's one-child policies, it will still dwarf the corresponding pool of potential American soldiers.

sive. We will return to the idea of an alternative posture for U.S. sea power in the Western Pacific.

Facing unfavorable trends in the regional military balance, the United States might be constrained to rely increasingly on its ability to deter China from using force by confronting it with expected costs that exceed expected gains. However, this path is also risky for the United States. In classical deterrence theory, even if the expected costs of escalation exceed the adversary's expected gains from aggression, the credibility of the threat to escalate, on which deterrence depends, can be undermined if the adversary suspects that escalation can also impose unacceptable costs on the side making the threat. In that case, deterrence can fail, leaving the side making the threat with a hard choice between escalating and having its bluff called, which can have its own severe costs.

In the case of conflict with China, the option of *vertical escalation* is increasingly risky for the United States because it entails moving to levels of hostilities—e.g., cyber-war, ASAT war, economic war, or, most extreme, nuclear war—at which China is becoming more capable and the United States is thus becoming more vulnerable to Chinese retaliation.[12]

Another U.S. option is *horizontal escalation*—expanding the geographic scope of a conflict, and by threatening to do so deterring the conflict in the first place. A version of this that gets attention among U.S. strategists from time to time is to cut off China's oil supply by intercepting tankers en route to Chinese ports, thus strangling China's economy. Other versions would have U.S. forces targeting a range of Chinese military, naval, or economic assets beyond the theater of military operations, and by threatening to do so give China pause before committing aggression. Such options as these could be credible in that China, lacking worldwide military capabilities, is far more vulnerable than the United States. However, China could choose to retaliate in other ways, e.g., cyber-war against the American economy or missile

---

[12] See David C. Gompert and Phillip Saunders, *The Paradox of Power: Sino-American Strategic Restraint in an Age of Vulnerability*, Washington, D.C.: National Defense University Press, 2011.

attacks on Japan. Moreover, cutting off China's oil supply or attacking Chinese economic targets could damage the East Asian and world economies, set bad precedents, and even raise questions about respect for the laws of war. Horizontal escalation is a path the United States would take only in the case of large and unambiguous Chinese aggression against a U.S. ally or vital U.S. interests, e.g., an attack on Japan or invasion of South Korea, which are very remote contingencies. Because the United States should not threaten any action that it is not prepared to take, it should be judicious in warning of horizontal escalation. Moreover, by bandying notions of such escalation as cutting off China's oil, the United States would confirm precisely what the Chinese fear and suspect: that American sea power is inherently threatening and so must be challenged.

Generally speaking, while the United States should not rule out vertical or horizontal escalation options, neither should it count on them. As defense against Chinese aggression in East Asia becomes more problematic, deterrence has to be strengthened. In general, it should disabuse the Chinese of the assumption that war with the United States would be easy or even possible to contain. But threats of escalation carry high costs: They could feed Chinese paranoia, cause China to enhance its own capabilities to escalate, and have consequences on the United States, if forced to escalate, that might outweigh its interests in a conflict.

In sum, U.S. strategy faces multiple quandaries in East Asia: It must restrain the use of Chinese military power without stimulating the growth of Chinese military power; reassure regional friends despite increasing risks to its force; and strengthen deterrence without counting on threats of escalation that it would not want to carry out, may not be credible, and would confirm Chinese suspicions of U.S. ill intentions.

On top of these quandaries, there is one more: countering China in the region while calling on China to partner with the United States in meeting global challenges. True, the Chinese have their own interests in stemming nuclear proliferation, defeating violent extremism, reducing dependence on Middle Eastern oil, and slowing climate change; so they might be willing to cooperate on these matters regardless of muscular U.S. forces in China's vicinity. Indeed, there is now modest but growing Sino-U.S. collaboration on such systemic problems even as competition in East Asia has intensified. At the same time, the Chinese have repeatedly shown a predilection to let the United States bear the costs and risks of meeting global challenges while they pursue their parochial national interests—that is, "free-ridership."[13] The importance of future China's cooperation in global security should not be underestimated. With its massive consumption of resources, including oil from Iran and ores from North Korea, skepticism about international pressure on despotic regimes, rising influence in the developing world, and permanent seat on the UN Security Council, China can frustrate or facilitate important U.S. security policies.

Given that Chinese and American interests tend to diverge regionally and converge globally, U.S. strategy must provide for both regional security and global collaboration. It can do this, in theory, by combining the deterrence of China with the engagement of China. This approach is fundamentally different, more complex, and more difficult than U.S. anti-Soviet strategy, which combined static containment and gradual wearing-down of a patently hostile, expansionist, and isolated opponent saddled with a doomed economic system and a bloated state. With China, the United States depends increasingly on the cooperation of a power that may at the same time endanger the stability and security of a vital region. Moreover, although the United States learned to live with a divided Europe, at great pain, it hardly wants an Asia divided between a U.S. bloc and China, much less all under China's influence.

Whether a U.S. strategy of countering China regionally and partnering with it globally is feasible remains unclear. Both governments will be driven by the need for domestic consensus toward a relationship more simply adversarial or else cooperative in nature. Yet, its interests require the United States to straddle the two components, which is more or less what it is now trying to do. If and as the strategy works, the United States could shift its weight toward cooperation, Sino-

---

[13] For example, with sanctions on Iran and in keeping petroleum sources and transport routes secure.

American relations should improve, and East Asia should be secure. If not, U.S. weight should shift toward deterrence.

U.S. military strategy in East Asia could be the most challenging aspect of this straddling-act. It will affect Chinese perceptions of U.S. intentions and thus affect Chinese behavior, whether by channeling Chinese policy toward moderation or by provoking the Chinese toward confrontation. Increased reliance on fixed forward forces for direct defense would ignore their declining survivability, stimulate a further Chinese military build-up, and spoil chances for Sino-U.S. global cooperation. Yet U.S. failure to deter China, support allies, and maintain freedom of access in the region would imperil stability and U.S. interests regionally and, given Asia's importance, globally.

The worsening vulnerability problem dictates changes in U.S. military posture in East Asia, stressing mobile joint forces that can be deployed virtually anywhere quickly, disperse without sacrificing the ability to concentrate force, and elude and flummox Chinese C4ISR (more on this later). Given the pitfalls of forward deployment of large-scale U.S. forces, let alone warfare with China on the Asian continent, improving the *local* defense capabilities should be an integral part of U.S. strategy. While the United States should not try to encircle China, the strengthening of allied defenses could reduce Chinese confidence in using force. The United States also must strive to retain its advantage in exploiting technology in order to stay a move ahead of Chinese force improvements, e.g., by shifting to less visible strike platforms while China is shoveling resources into targeting the old ones. Such a posture could make it easier—though never easy—for an American president to order U.S. forces to be sent and used in regional contingencies, thus enhancing deterrence and the ability to manage crises involving China. (More on an alternative U.S. force posture later.)

Even a posture that avoids the pitfalls of large-scale forward defense must work with and not at cross-purposes to the desire for Chinese cooperation. With both U.S. and increasingly capable Chinese forces operating in the same geographic space, there may be more danger of conflict due to miscalculation or mistake than due to intention. This suggests a need for open, timely communications and military-to-military contact between the two—better yet, military-to-military cooperation. Chinese suspicions of U.S. intentions and doubtful civilian control of the PLA will make military-to-military progress difficult, yet also more important. The United States will want to avoid provocative actions unless critical for U.S. security—e.g., avoid blatantly threatening exercises and non-essential probes near recognized Chinese territory. Doing this while maintaining allied confidence and deterring China will take wise military leadership and close coordination with U.S. policymaking.

American Sea Power in the Western Pacific

In geo-economic terms, East Asia is a sprawling archipelago that extends from Japan to Malaysia to New Zealand and includes Eastern China. Trade with and throughout the archipelago is all sea-borne. In addition, the waters of the archipelago are abundant with food and fuel, and control of them is increasingly contested. Because the region lives around, on, and from the sea, the ability of the United States to maintain economic access, stability, and influence there depends on its sea power.

If it lacked sea power, the United States could not assure freedom of passage in East Asian international waters, nor prevent China from controlling at least the South China Sea if not also the East China Sea and Yellow Sea. Sea power enables the United States to back up friendly regional states in resisting whatever pressure China might exert. In the event of hostilities, sea power would enable the United States to conduct effective strike, expeditionary, and reinforcement operations in most parts of the region. As forward U.S. air bases and fixed concentrations of forces near China become more vulnerable, the mobility inherent in sea power becomes more essential. Geo-politically, because sea power has symbolized the commitment of the United States to regional stability for nearly a century, its weakening would be interpreted by allies and China alike as the precursor of a Chinese sphere of influence, which the United States cannot tolerate.

At present, American sea power has two core missions in the Western Pacific—one operational and one political. The operational mission is to *strike*. The political mission is to *influence* friends and foes in peacetime or crisis. The main instrument of both operational strike and political influence has been the large carrier.[14] Sure enough, the large carrier has become the bull's-eye for China's defense investments and targeting.

Because current technology does not hold out a realistic promise of being able to defend a few large U.S. carriers from Chinese targeting, the United States must rethink the main instruments of its sea power in the Western Pacific. Its naval strategists must ask whether it remains wise, or even necessary, to heed Mahan's 19th-century maxim to consolidate offensive forces. If they do not ask this, U.S. sea power will not be able to meet the 21st-century Western Pacific demands of its core operational mission (to strike); as a consequence, its political mission (to influence) will also be in jeopardy. Although the United States has a decade or more before the current form of its sea power in the Western Pacific is obsolete, it will take at least as long to re-form that sea power, assuming the Navy has the ambition to do so.

Overall, the U.S. Navy has steadily declined in size over the past 20 years: from 590 ships in 1990 to 318 in 2000 to 288 in 2010.[15] With current U.S. defense budget projections, the Navy will be able to maintain no more than about 240 ships. This reduction in fleet size is the result of climbing costs of individual ships and, more recently, tight constraints on funding for ship-building because of the higher priority the United States has placed for the past decade on ground forces for large-scale ground occupations and operations.[16] In parallel, the absence of a major blue-water rival has weakened the case for maintaining a large U.S. fleet.

In addition to aircraft carriers, every other main category of U.S. sea power is active in the Western Pacific: surface combatants, auxiliary

---

[14] If in doubt about the centrality of the large aircraft carrier in the identity of the U.S. Navy, observe any recruiting advertisement: In essence, the carrier has become the symbol of the "Global Force for Good."

[15] Naval History and Heritage Command, 2011.

[16] The Navy has in effect helped to "pay the bill" for the expansion and continuous employment of U.S. ground forces under U.S. post-9/11 defense strategy.

ships, amphibious ships, attack submarines, strategic-deterrent submarines, and naval bases. A large fraction of the rest of the fleet—surface combatants, auxiliaries, attack submarines—exists and operates to provide anti-ship, anti-submarine, and anti-missile defense so that the carriers can carry out their strike mission. If the carriers' ability to carry out that mission is put in doubt, so is the principal rationale for much of the surface fleet.

To be sure, other naval missions are also important. As the United States reduces its strategic offensive nuclear forces, the submarine-based missile force, though also reduced, becomes more important because of its superior survivability, given the difficulty of finding and sinking submarines. In addition, the United States is improving the conventional strike capability of surface combatants and submarines, including converted strategic boats, with extended-range cruise and ballistic missiles. Meant to complement the strike power of large aircraft carriers, such capabilities will become more important as the carriers become more vulnerable.

Make no mistake: As this is written, the United States enjoys naval preponderance globally and in the Western Pacific. It is utterly unrivaled on the high seas, it can operate well in coastal waters, and it can control whatever maritime choke-points it is tasked to secure. This current supremacy is a consequence of not only the extraordinary capabilities of the ships of the fleet, but also the Navy's progress in networking them for better offense and defense. It reflects as well the fact that few other countries can afford capital-intensive, fuel-guzzling blue-water navies; most of those that can are U.S. partners—Japan, European allies, India. In the Western Pacific and elsewhere, American sea power is both unrivaled and supplemented in sheer numbers and operational strength by the sea power of others.

Still, the vulnerability of concentrated American sea power in the Western Pacific presents a specific problem of great geo-political, geo-economic, and potentially war-fighting significance. We have established that East Asia is too important for the United States to accept a Chinese sphere of influence there, which the weakening of U.S. sea power would do. But history shows that the weakening of one *form* of sea power does not necessarily amount to the weakening of sea power itself; rather, it leads to new forms by exploiting new technology: wood to iron, sail to steam, battleships to aircraft carriers, surface ships to submarines, bombs to missiles, manned aircraft to drones, signal flags and smoke signals to radio to worldwide space-based data communications.

In addition to rethinking the *form* of American sea power in the Western Pacific, it is time also to reflect on its *meaning*. Because the United States believes it needs assured maritime freedom in the region, it must be able to maintain sea control and prevent Chinese sea denial. But this does not necessarily mean that the United States must maintain the ability to deny China access to the seas on which *its* economy depends. If denying China access were the ultimate U.S. goal, it is virtually certain that China, being vitally dependent on the seas, would do whatever it took to challenge it. Recall that when it became clear to the Japanese that the United States intended to exercise sea denial, they were willing not only to commit vast resources but also to start a war to prevent it. The Sino-American case is further complicated by China's need for access to resources in and under the seas.

Short of outright Chinese aggression in East Asia, akin to Japanese aggression in the 1930s, the United States is unlikely to declare sea denial as its purpose. At the same time, there is enough unofficial U.S. chatter about the option of blockading or severing China's sea lifelines in a crisis, that the Chinese could be worried already about U.S. sea-denial aims. If they conclude that this is what the United States intends, the result will be intensified naval competition, improved and expanded Chinese anti-naval capabilities, a worsening of Sino-American relations, an increased potential for confrontation, and a rising risk of miscalculations, mistakes, and inadvertent war.

Mahan's formula was that global power requires sea power, sea power excites rivalry, rivalry demands the ability to deny the other's use of the sea, rivalry can lead to war, and victory depends on concentrated offensive force. But that formula contains assumptions that are not necessarily valid in these waters, in this century, between these two powers—and, because of China's potential and its own need for oceanic access, may impose prohibitive costs and risks on the United States. Of course, whether it is possible for the United States to retain and fulfill the main purposes of sea power in the Western Pacific without intensifying rivalry with China depends as much on China as it does on the United States.

Chinese Interests[17]

Starting with Deng Xiaoping (1904–1997), China's political leaders have worked to transform it from a poor, unstable, weak, vulnerable, and pitied country into a prosperous, stable, strong, secure, and influential one. Whether the prime motivation has been to take better care of a billion Chinese, to make China more cohesive, to end foreign domination once and for all, or to reclaim China's greatness is unclear—and may not really matter, because these aims are correlated. The path to achieving them all is economic development. Development relieves the grinding poverty of the masses and increases Chinese power, security, and clout. It also assures domestic political calm, thus the survival of the regime.

The course Deng set reflects and reinforces a way of thinking about China's needs and purposes that was fundamentally new. Communist ideology, which obviously was not helping China, gave way to an ideology of state-sponsored economic growth. This necessitated the granting of considerable economic freedom. But economic freedom was not to be accompanied by political freedom: Chinese communism has shed its Marxist economics but not its Maoist resolve to rule unchallenged. Authoritarianism is claimed by those who practice it as a prerequisite of growth. While this is a questionable theory—contradicted by the parallel development and democratization of numerous other peoples in recent decades—there is no doubt that growth, thus satisfying the needs of the people, is a prerequisite of preserving the political status quo. Instead of demanding reform, much less brewing revolution, China's middle class is more or less content with the political status quo. Moreover, those who have gained the most are especially proud of China's achievements and of the mind that China should

[17] This analysis of Chinese interests makes use of unpublished RAND research by Eric Heginbotham, cited with the author's consent.

assert its expanding interests and influence in the region and the world. Economically and politically, China's success makes it both able and inclined to be and act the great power.

The model for Chinese development is not unlike that followed by a number of other East Asian states: acquire the capital and know-how to employ low-cost labor in manufacturing; attain superior productivity by training and organizing that labor; work up the value-chain from commodity to more profitable production; export strategically (with state support) into global markets so that domestic production is not held back by domestic consumption; keep currency exchange rates low, run surpluses, and amass foreign exchange; with that foreign exchange, buy the raw materials, equipment, and technology needed to sustain growth; allow yet control foreign investment in the growing domestic market in order to acquire the means to compete in foreign markets; expand free enterprise, but keep the state's hand in businesses that matter most.[18] But China's version of the model has differed from other East Asian states in two respects. First, its huge rural population, engaged largely in subsistence farming, has enabled it to add hundreds of millions of low-wage production workers and thus to become a market-share leader in manufacturing for the world economy. Second, while development spurred political reform in most other East Asian states, it has not thus far in China.[19]

China's development has both required and deepened integration into the world economy and dependence on overseas markets and raw materials. While the Chinese will not be able to keep GDP growth at the 10 percent per annum of the past two decades, they may be able to keep it at 6–8 percent (which is still extraordinary for such a large economy). Conversely, it is widely thought that substantially slower growth could endanger the regime's ability to meet rising expectations and thus maintain unchallenged one-party rule. It follows that China's access to markets and materials, nearly all by sea, is a matter of considerable political interest to the regime. "Leaders in Beijing see social

---

18 For example, defense, energy, finance.

19 Samantha Ravitch, *Marketization and Democracy: East Asian Experiences*, New York: Cambridge University Press, 1999.

instability as the greatest threat to themselves and balanced economic development and growth as central social stability. Indeed, they often discuss a critical benchmark, believing that 7 percent growth is necessary to support a growing pool of urban workers."[20] The security of sea-borne trade is also crucial to China's increasingly powerful business community and well-connected, well-heeled tycoons.

China's development strategy necessitated a fundamental change in its foreign policy that prevails to this day. Knowing that trade would be crucial to provide jobs, Deng jettisoned Mao's interest in stirring up revolution abroad in favor of doing business with established regimes in the region and beyond.[21] If pre-growth China rejected the international system on grounds of socialist ideology, the ideology of growth has required China to accept and join the system. By the same token, the Chinese understand that growth based on international trade argues for international peace and against subverting or threatening other states, especially key trading partners (including its neighbors). It argues as well for keeping the medium of trade—the oceans—tranquil and secure. China's need for stability implies a convergence of its global interests with those of the United States and its partners.

In addition to the need for overseas trade, China's development strategy depends on the acquisition of technology, which is to be found in the United States, Japan, and the rest of the capitalist West. Thus, the combination of American consumers' bottomless appetite for low-cost goods and Chinese producers' requirement for manufacturing technology has made Sino-U.S. economic cooperation highly beneficial, as detailed earlier. China and the United States have benefited enormously not only from their bilateral cooperation but also from the general expansion of trade and investment that characterize global eco-

---

[20] Heginbotham, unpublished RAND research.

[21] According to Heginbotham (unpublished RAND research): "Emblematic of Deng Xiaoping's pragmatism and his focus on increasing Chinese trade, Deng's most important statement on foreign policy (and the one most frequently quoted in China) ended with the admonition to 'keep a low profile and achieve something.' In the jostling over Chinese foreign policy today, Deng's comment continues to be advanced by those who believe that China remains underdeveloped and that trade and economic growth should remain the paramount focus of its foreign policy."

nomic integration. Both depend on the health of the world economy, on international stability in general, and on the multilateral institutions and rules of this order.

But before jumping to the conclusion that this convergence of interests precludes rivalry between the rising power and the established power of today, remember that Great Britain and Imperial Germany also had common economic interests yet went to war. Indeed, now that China's success enables it to pursue its *other* national interests—defense, sovereign integrity, unification, and influence—there is a growing potential for friction and conflict between China and its neighbors, who are supported by the United States. Having been weak and vulnerable for so long, the Chinese definition of national defense begins with the protection of China proper. While the threat of re-armed Japan is dormant, or done, it is still not dismissed by the Chinese because of their brutal treatment by the Japanese in the 1930s and 1940s.[22] One might think that the Chinese would be careful not to stimulate Japan's military expansion by appearing threatening. Instead, the Chinese have used their new capabilities and confidence to challenge Japan in the East China Sea and have reacted harshly, and nationalistically, to Japan's increasingly tough defense policy.

Of greater and more immediate concern, of course, is the danger the Chinese perceive of U.S. military power, including sea-based strike power, in the Western Pacific. With the Soviet Union gone and Japanese expansionism long gone, the Chinese now want U.S. power to recede. While Americans are concerned by China's development of A2AD capabilities, the Chinese can claim that not developing these capabilities, now that they can, would be irresponsible. They can also

---

[22] Heginbotham (unpublished RAND research) observes that when tensions with Japan boiled over in 2005, Chinese activists pressured the government to take a tougher line against Tokyo on historical and UN-related issues. Following a relatively standard script, the government allowed some protests to occur, while mobilizing its community of Japan specialists to tour campuses, trade groups, and other organizations to dampen tensions and encourage an end to activism, largely on the grounds that stable trade and investment relations with Japan are critical to China's interests, whereas addressing other political disputes will take more time.

ask why the United States is committed to keep its military power in the region unless to threaten China.

The Chinese view of national security does not end with defense of the mainland against attack. China's definition of national sovereignty and territorial integrity is being applied more widely to include the control of Taiwan. The growth of Chinese power has made more realistic the goal of Taiwan's reunification, as well as the imperative of preventing Taiwan's independence. Since the earliest days of the People's Republic, the Chinese have seen the United States and its sea power as the principal barrier to forcible reunification. In 1996, when U.S. aircraft carriers entered the Strait to prevent China's intimidation of Taiwan, the Chinese were reminded of their impotence to overcome this barrier. While the Chinese have serious misgivings about actually taking Taiwan by force, their inability to do so denies them the upper hand in cross-Strait negotiations. Although, as noted, China-Taiwan relations are progressing, the Chinese still regard U.S. willingness to intervene in Taiwan's defense as a contradiction of one of its core interests.

Apart from its assertion of sovereignty over Taiwan, China has numerous other territorial claims. It has settled or deferred most of its land-border disputes, which may signify its interest in a stable neighborhood as it re-orients strategically toward the Pacific and its most formidable potential adversary, the United States.[23] While deferring its land-territorial claims, China has become more adamant, impatient, and rowdy over its maritime-territorial claims. Of the latter, the most consequential economically and for regional security are those in the South China Sea. While China's political leaders have not asserted that these interests are of the same order as its control over Taiwan and Tibet, military officers have intimated that Chinese sovereignty is at stake, implying that these are not just Chinese claims but sovereign rights with which others in the area are interfering.[24] In any case, China's interests in controlling the South China Sea is at odds with

---

[23] Taylor Fravel, *Strong Borders, Secure Nation: Cooperation and Conflict in China's Territorial Disputes*, Princeton: Princeton University Press, 2008.

[24] Heginbotham, unpublished RAND research.

its interests in maintaining friendly and influential relations with its Southeast Asian neighbors.[25]

Chinese policy statements continue to recognize international stability as a precondition for economic growth based on trade. As China's neighbors have become wary of its power, Beijing has adopted such formulations as "peaceful rise" and "peace and development." On the whole, China has used its growing clout judiciously and been a stalwart supporter of the sanctity of existing sovereigns, regardless of their legitimacy (or regarding them as legitimate by definition). It has generally opposed economic sanctions and international intervention. It is often at loggerheads with the United States and its allies over regime change (e.g., in the Middle East) and the "responsibility to protect" (e.g., in Africa), partly because of its attachment to the principle of noninterference and partly to protect its access to established regimes and their energy and other resources.

Compared with Imperial Germany, Imperial Japan, and Teddy Roosevelt's acquisitive America, China has been the model of restraint. Whereas they colonialized in order to get resources (and for other reasons), China relies instead on development aid, trading leverage, investment, and preferential long-term supply contracts, without attaching strings to such issues as the way a regime treats its people. China's record of military action during its economic expansion since the 1980s pales in comparison with that of the United States, which has used significant force in Panama, Kuwait, Bosnia, Kosovo, Iraq, Afghanistan, and Libya during that same period. Far from being belligerent, revisionist, or revolutionary, China has actually been conservative and reserved internationally.[26]

---

[25] Deng's admonition to avoid international trouble, for the sake of development, has been employed in explicit opposition to Beijing's assertiveness on the South China Sea. Heginbotham, unpublished RAND research.

[26] China has been an active participant in the six-party talks on North Korea and has participated in anti-piracy missions in the Gulf of Aden, creating joint patrols with South Korean and Japanese contingents. On some economic trade and investment issues, its position is often closer to that of the United States than, for example, India. In other cases, Chinese positions conflict with those of the United States. On issues that relate to sovereignty norms—for example, sanctions against Egypt, Syria, or Iran—China has sided with Russia,

Will China's caution decline as its ability to act militarily grows? This is unclear, for China's interests pull it in two different directions: multilateral-cooperative and unilateral-assertive. Its need for access to materials and markets—to sustain economic development and political stability—creates contradictory impulses. Again, it has benefited from and has a continuing interest in a healthy and well-managed world economy, a quiet and peaceful international environment, good standing with states near and far, open and secure international waters, and avoiding conflict and costly arms competition with the United States. Yet, the magnitude and urgency of China's economic demands lead it to seek unilateral advantage (e.g., in preferential long-term energy supply relationships), to stay on good terms with bad regimes sitting on resources (Iranian oil, Sudanese oil, North Korean ores), and even to threaten force to back its positions in disputes with large economic stakes (e.g., in the South China Sea). China favors and complies with rules, unless it can do better by skirting them while others comply.

The Chinese impulse to act unilaterally and forcefully appears to be stronger the closer to China one gets. Generally, China favors "soft power" globally and "hard power" regionally. It is unclear whether this is because China has growing regional yet scant global military capabilities, because its interests are stronger—worth fighting for—the nearer they are, or because it seeks some degree of regional dominance. For our purposes, what matters is that China appears willing and is increasingly able to threaten force to advance and defend its interests in a region that is too important for the United States to grant China the prerogative to do so. While Great Britain was ready to grant such a prerogative to the United States in the Western Hemisphere in the late 19th century, the United States appears willing to give China no such space today. The two questions this leaves, then, are: Which

---

Brazil, India, and others in opposing U.S. and European efforts (or supporting significantly watered-down versions). And while China is a member of most of the organizations that define the world system today, it is also an active and important participant in at least two organizations—the Shanghai Cooperation Organization (SCO) and the Brazil, Russia, India, China, and South Africa (BRICS) group—that have tried to push the international system in directions more amenable to developing or non-Western states. Heginbotham, unpublished RAND research.

great power will be more capable militarily in the Western Pacific? (see Chapter Four) and Will the interaction of U.S. and Chinese interests and capabilities in the Western Pacific necessarily be confrontational? (see Chapter Five).

Having identified the seeds of Sino-U.S. rivalry and potential confrontation in the Western Pacific, it is important to note that the compatibility of Chinese and U.S. interests globally could have a moderating effect, on both countries, in the region. As noted in the preceding discussion of U.S. interests, Chinese and U.S. interests are more conducive to cooperation beyond than in East Asia. Notwithstanding their criticism of U.S. unilateralism and preference for multi-polarity, the Chinese are generally comfortable with the current global order, which has served them well. China shares U.S. interests in the free flow of goods, capital, and technology; containment of extremism; security of energy sources and routes; reduction of poverty; peaceful resolution of disputes; and control of nuclear weapons. While China often disagrees with the United States outside of East Asia—notably, on the issue of intervention—this has not prevented cooperation on other global issues nor brought them anywhere close to hostilities (for which, as noted, the United States has overwhelming advantages). Fundamentally, China's congeniality on global issues is not a favor or concession to the United States but instead a pursuit of Chinese interests that happen to coincide with U.S. interests. It follows that China could remain cooperative elsewhere while competing regionally. At the same time, like the United States', China's interest and involvement in global cooperation may curb its regional antagonism.

Yet, as noted earlier, there is some possibility of Sino-American confrontation in all of East Asia's potential trouble hot spots: Korea, Taiwan, the South China Sea, the East China Sea, and China's land dispute with Vietnam. Arching over these particular dangers is China's intent to reduce the U.S. threat to itself and to the pursuit of its regional interests. Moreover, whether or not it means to achieve some sort of regional hegemony, China's interest in access to the world's resources, its markets, and thus its oceans, place it at odds with the U.S. presence off its shores. Because the Chinese regard U.S. military and naval capabilities in the region as a potential danger to their interests, they feel the need to challenge the dominant sea power in the Western Pacific, and they are working energetically to meet that need with their anti-naval capabilities.

Chinese Strategy

The tensions that define U.S. strategy toward China likewise define Chinese strategy toward the United States in particular and the outside world in general: To gain economic access and earn influence within the existing order and or to use its mounting power unilaterally. To keep the external environment calm or to press Chinese rights and claims. To befriend neighbors or to encourage deference to Chinese might, at the risk of isolation. To pursue good relations with the United States or to undermine U.S. power and influence where it could harm Chinese interests. To avoid a costly arms race or to seek operational-military advantages to deter or defeat threats to China and its interests. To rely on the United States and on cooperation with it to keep trade routes secure or to build and deploy capabilities to do so independently. Like the United States, the Chinese will try to have it both ways on these choices.

As noted, the impulses, constraints, and choices of Chinese strategy will differ from East Asia to the world at large. Cooperation is more appealing globally; competition more compelling regionally. The farther from China, the less capability and latitude for risk-taking the Chinese have.[27] When the security of China and its sovereign interests, e.g., reunification and territorial rights, is at stake, the Chinese are less willing to leave outcomes to others. When they are constrained to negotiate and seek agreed solutions bearing on those sovereign interests, the Chinese will exploit the shadow of their growing military power if

---

[27] Heginbotham (unpublished RAND research) notes that, on the global stage, China would like to be seen as an important and constructive member of international society, though there is much ambivalence about exactly what that means. It has a great stake in much of the current architecture of global governance and values its position within the United Nations and UN Security Council, World Trade Organization, G-20, NPT Nuclear Suppliers' Group, and a host of other international organizations.

not the threat of force. As Chinese interests and defensive concerns become less acute at greater distance—in the Middle East and Africa, for example—the shadow vanishes and cooperation is more likely. In the Western Indian Ocean, for example, the Chinese navy works with those of the Americans, Japanese, South Koreans, and others to protect international shipping from Somali pirates. Yet in the Western Pacific, Chinese ships harass some of those same navies.

Is the contrast between Chinese regional and global behavior the result of a contrast between its near and far military capabilities or instead a matter of strategy reflecting a difference in importance between its near and far interests? The answer is probably both: China is more advanced in developing and deploying regional military capabilities than global ones because the former are easier, cheaper, quicker, and in some ways a logical step toward the latter. But regional military capabilities are also a much higher priority, driven largely by considerations of the defense of China itself. Generally, as states extend their definitions of security from their territory to their interests abroad, their military capabilities are also extended, unless of course they lack the resources or are content to count on the strength, or good behavior, of others. Though amply resourced, it is not clear that the Chinese want to invest heavily in the ability to station or project forces around the world if they can count on others, mainly the United States, to look after Chinese interests.

The role of military forces generally in China's strategy bears examination. Having treated defense spending as a low priority when the country was struggling to escape mass poverty and build national infrastructure, the Chinese have in the past decade made military capabilities a high priority. Past growth in spending on defense has matched GDP growth at roughly 10 percent. But in the past few years, Chinese defense spending has grown faster than GDP—as high as 18 percent per annum. As a result, China now spends as much on defense as the rest of East Asia combined (excluding North Korea). China's estimated 2011 defense spending was $130 billion; the next six totaled $128 billion.[28] Assuming present growth rates and that Japan stays near its traditional 1 percent of GDP for defense, Chinese military spending will be twice that of the region in as little as five years.

Chinese defense spending today is dwarfed by that of the United States. However, if current trends continue, this gap will shrink in both absolute and relative terms, as Figure 1 shows. Of significance is that the preponderance of Chinese military investments and activities will be concentrated in East Asia, whereas the United States must meet global demands. During the post-9/11 decade, at least 40 percent of U.S. defense spending could be attributed to meeting the needs of the U.S. Central Command (CENTCOM), compared with roughly 20 percent for the U.S. Pacific Command (PACOM), the second-biggest claimant.[29] Even if and as the United States shifts its defense priori-

Figure 1
Projected Defense Spending for China, Japan, and the United States Through 2040

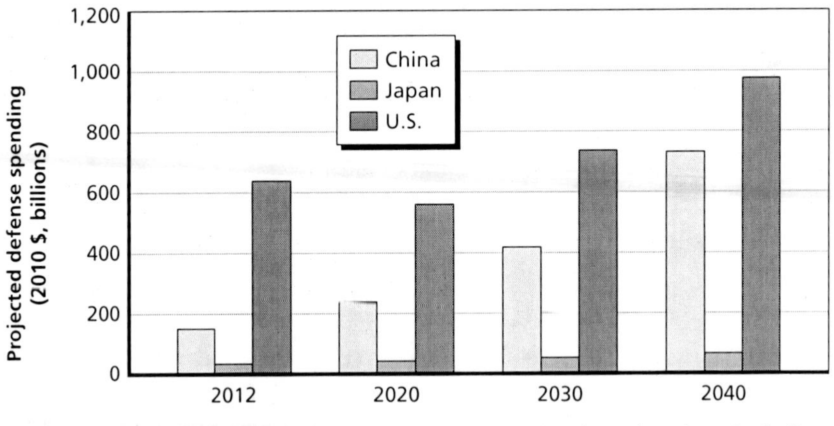

SOURCE: James Dobbins, David C. Gompert, David A. Shlapak, and Andrew Scobell, *Conflict with China: Prospects, Consequences, and Strategies for Deterrence*, Santa Monica, Calif.: RAND Corporation, OP-344, 2011.

RAND *RR151-1*

---

28 Japan, $55 billion; South Korea, $28 billion; Australia, $23 billion; Singapore, $9 billion; Taiwan, $8 billion; Indonesia, $5 billion.

29 David C. Gompert, Paul K. Davis, Stuart E. Johnson, and Duncan Long: *Analysis of Strategy and Strategies of Analysis*, Santa Monica, Calif.: RAND Corporation, MG-718-JS, 2008.

ties to East Asia, it is most unlikely that it will be able to match China's future spending directed toward the region. To illustrate crudely, based on these aggregate projections, and assuming that 33 percent of U.S. defense spending is to support PACOM and 66 percent of Chinese spending is directed to PACOM's area, China will outspend the United States and Japan together on military capabilities and activities in East Asia over the next 20 years.

The growth in China's defense outlays has gone overwhelmingly toward building up its Pacific-oriented capabilities. There are several reasons for this: the priority placed on self-defense; preoccupation with neutralizing U.S. strike capabilities in the region; the need to back up Chinese territorial claims; and the simple fact that air, naval, and force-projection capabilities increase in cost as a function of range (making regional ones affordable and extra-regional ones not). However, the fact that China has placed its emphasis almost exclusively on regional capabilities confirms the predisposition toward hard power in the region and soft power beyond that one can observe.

Just as the United States defines security in terms of interests, including but going well beyond its territory, China may move in this direction. Like the United States, it has the economic wherewithal and worldwide interests to do so. The difference between the two is not only a matter of being at different stages of development but also one of geography: The United States has not been concerned with the military presence in its region of any other power since the Cold War (and before then, in the 19th century), whereas China is very concerned with the presence of another power, the United States, in its region. Just as the United States sought to banish Spanish, British, and the Soviet power from its region, Chinese strategy is to pressure American power in its region.

At the same time, China is neither blatantly aggressive nor categorically hostile to U.S. interests in East Asia. The goal of securing what it regards as sovereign territory is in tension with the need to maintain good relations with its neighbors and the United States. In the face of confrontational Chinese behavior in the South China Sea in the 1990s, regional states sought closer military ties with the United States. China responded by launching a "charm offensive" to prevent

U.S. alliances from being strengthened and itself from being isolated. In recent years, China has again become pushy, especially with regard to maritime-boundary disputes with its Southeast Asia neighbors. Similar swings can be seen in China's relations with Japan, South Korea, and Taiwan. Because of this experience and China's steady military build-up, the important states of the Western Pacific are less susceptible to Chinese charm.

Despite such political backlash in the region, and because of the perceived U.S. threat, the Chinese are unlikely to gravitate toward an accommodating, soft-power strategy in the region, as they are doing beyond the region. Whether the United States has been sufficiently consistent and creative in drawing China into cooperative solutions to East Asian problems is a policy matter to which we will return in Chapter Five. Under current conditions, the United States cannot assume that China will cease to strengthen its A2AD capabilities, forgo threats to get its way in territorial disputes, or accept strong U.S. military presence.

The apparent commitment of China to strengthen its regional military capabilities raises the question of the purposes to which these capabilities might be put. Again, there is no indication that China wants to conquer neighboring nation-states. Nor is there logic to such Chinese designs, given the integration of East Asian economies. The ideology of growth—as opposed to that of messianic revolution—requires and has succeeded in providing access to foreign resources through trade, investment, and correct state-to-state relations. Although China has several contested borders, as well as 100 million or more ethnic Chinese living in the region outside of China, it is hard to see how the benefits of wholesale territorial conquest would be worth the staggering costs and the risks of a conflagration. More plausible is that the Chinese would use force against neighbors to settle prejudicially territorial disputes that involve important Chinese interests, such as achieving national unification or securing access to essential sea-based resources. Also plausible is China's use of force in the event it feels threatened, such as in the event of a violent collapse of the North Korean state, the loss of control over North Korean nuclear weapons, or South Korean incursion into North Korea. The form this might take is at this point unclear, and whether Chinese military intervention in North Korea would be harmful or helpful depends on circumstances and on Chinese aims.

If Chinese strategy includes options of using force for such purposes, the PLA must plan for contingencies involving hostilities with intervening U.S. forces. As already discussed, important U.S. interests and commitments would be at stake in the event of Chinese use of force against Taiwan, in the South China Sea, against Japan in the East China Sea, or against South Korea. Therefore, the PLA's ability to deter or degrade U.S. military intervention in the Western Pacific is a necessary component of Chinese strategy—again, even in the absence of Chinese designs to conquer any neighboring nation-states. This is something to which the Chinese military, with the blessing of the political leadership, has given a great deal of attention; indeed, it is central to Chinese military strategy and priorities. Moreover, even if China opts not to use its growing power to get its way in regional quarrels, the presence of U.S. strike forces hardens its resolve to neutralize this threat-in-being.

Before Deng, China quarreled mainly with its land neighbors: India, Vietnam, and the Soviet Union. Since Deng, China's access to the Pacific and the world beyond has become far more important than its exact boundaries in remote and non-useful hinterlands of Asia. In addition, China's rise has increased the feasibility of Taiwan's re-unification; while the Chinese do not want to use force for this purpose, their ability to do so could be essential to gaining enough leverage to produce a favorable outcome politically. Whether in anticipating a conflict over Taiwan or in assuring Chinese access to the Pacific, U.S. military power, especially U.S. sea power, could be a major obstacle. Add to these concerns the potential threat to China of U.S. strike power in the Western Pacific, and one sees why Chinese strategy requires plans and preparations for military conflict with the United States—hardly what the Chinese want, but something that circumstance might force on them.

Chinese military strategy to thwart U.S. intervention has been extensively documented, even advertised by the Chinese, and exhaustively analyzed by the Americans.[30] In a nutshell, Chinese military strategists believe the PLA's best chance of deterring, degrading, or defeating U.S. intervention is to strike U.S. intervention forces swiftly, perhaps preemptively, and to limit as much as possible the ensuing conflict's scope—duration, geography, weapons, targets, damage. This strategy explains the priority the PLA places on A2AD capabilities. In its sights are the most likely instruments of U.S. intervention: large aircraft carriers. To target the carriers, the Chinese are developing extended-range and space-based sensors, space-based guidance systems, anti-ship ballistic missiles, cruise missiles, attack submarines, and digital communications networks to tie everything together. Chinese doctrine calls for swift, intense, coordinated attacks to impede and degrade U.S. forces. While not seeking armed conflict with the United States, obviously, Chinese military strategy depends on attacking U.S. strike forces early, first, or even preemptively if conflict appears probable.

Even with such capabilities and doctrine, the PLA cannot expect to prevent successful U.S. military intervention unless (a) U.S. political leaders decide that the costs and risks outweigh the value of intervention; (b) hostilities remain confined in scope and end before the United States can bring its global strike power to bear; or (c) the command, control, and communications systems on which U.S. forces vitally depend are crippled. Because the Chinese cannot be confident of the first or second factor, both being mainly under U.S. control, they have begun to concentrate on the third. The PLA's interest in both cyberwarfare and anti-satellite warfare is driven by the belief that its best and perhaps only chance of prevailing against U.S. forces is to attack U.S. space-based and other command, control, and communications networks, which are relatively vulnerable. (We will return to military-technological competition and its effect on possible Sino-U.S. conflict in the next chapter.)

Just as U.S. military strategy serves both operational and political needs, so does China's. The more capable the PLA is of conducting successful operations against its regional and U.S. forces, the longer and darker will be the shadow cast on relationships and actions short

[30] Among the latest and best examples is Saunders et al., 2011.

of war by all actors in the region. At the same time, the Chinese may feel pressure to "pull their punches"—at least in the use of force even in the forces they deploy—for fear of adverse political reactions. Again, if recent years are a guide to the future, the expansion and use of Chinese military capabilities has been attended not by greater regional deference but by the opposite: greater interest by U.S. allies and potential partners in a strong U.S. posture. There are sure to be some influential Chinese concerned that unreserved support for the PLA to satisfy its operational requirements would hurt, not help, China's political ambitions in the region.

Aside from its military aspects, Chinese strategy is more or less a mirror image of U.S. strategy: preparing for confrontation in East Asia in hopes of avoiding it, while cooperating where interests converge globally. Like the United States, China would suffer grievous economic damage in the event of regional conflict; and like the Americans, the Chinese no doubt think that this consideration will dictate caution on the part of its potential adversary. China's integration into the world economy is thus crucial not only for development but also in giving the United States a strong disincentive to use force against China, especially if it has no vital interests involved. In addition, China will partner with the United States on global challenges—nuclear nonproliferation, counterterrorism, counter-piracy, energy security—when it serves Chinese security interests and as long as the costs are not too high. It will also seek a greater voice and accept more responsibility in international institutions. Given its regional interests, China will need to balance cooperative global policies with assertive regional ones, just like the United States will. Taking a belligerent posture in East Asia could ruin prospects for global cooperation; yet taking a humble posture in East Asia in order to expand global cooperation would leave the United States in a position to threaten, intervene, and align the region against China.

While it would be a mistake to interpret Chinese strategy and predict Chinese behavior as a product of "hawks and doves" vying for or slicing up control, there is a pattern worth noting. Whereas the PLA is preoccupied with the security of China and preparations for conflict, the state's civilian leaders and institutions (e.g., the Ministry of Foreign Affairs) are also interested in improving China's standing in the world and relations with countries that can help it achieve its goals. With respect to the United States, the PLA has responsibility to plan for military contingencies, which are all in China's vicinity; the civilians are expected to maintain a stable international environment and to manage the complex mix of cooperative and competitive Sino-U.S. relations. On top of this, China's new business elites have a strong interest and some influence in creating favorable conditions for Chinese trade, investment, and acquisition of technology, in which the United States figures significantly. Finally, China's expanding numbers of informed citizens are showing increased pride, patriotism, and nationalism about China's success, its role in the world, and its relations with the United States. Ironically, the middle-class Chinese who have so much to gain from economic cooperation favor a hard line when China is disrespected by the Americans (or Japanese).

Reflecting the perspectives of its hawkish officers, cautious statesmen, internationalist businessmen, and nationalistic bourgeoisie, as well as tensions among its global and regional interests, China's strategy contains a mix of moderation and belligerence, making it all the more perplexing for the United States, just as U.S. strategy is obviously perplexing for the Chinese (and many Americans). Notwithstanding one-party rule, finding a genuine and stable synthesis among these competing interests and perspectives will be as difficult for China as it is for the United States. In quoting Deng Xiaoping's famous aphorism, high Chinese officials have modified the original: China should "*uphold* keeping a low profile and *actively* achieve something" (modifications in italics).[31] This implies that China can be more assertive abroad, as its power now permits, and still preserve a tranquil environment, as its development still demands.

Because of the internal tensions and lack of consensus in China's strategy, its conduct will be largely in reaction to challenges and opportunities presented by the United States. Steady pursuit by the United States of Sino-U.S. global economic and security partnership could embolden those in China who favor a moderate and multilateral

---

[31] M. Taylor Fravel, "Revising Deng's Foreign Policy," taylorfravel.com, January 17, 2012.

approach to the region. But by the same token, it would be a mistake for the United States to bank on Chinese politicians, much less generals and admirals, to embrace cooperation outside their region with a power seen as threatening to China and its interests in their region. Yet, for the United States to relinquish its role in East Asian security in the belief that Chinese strategy will become more cooperative might have the opposite effect. We will return to the question of the interaction of Chinese and U.S. strategy in the Western Pacific after analyzing what sea power means to the Chinese.

Chinese Sea Power

Mahan viewed China as an *object* of sea power. As an avid reader of world history, Mahan knew that China had not been a sea power since the early 15th century. As the 19th century ended, Great Britain, Japan, the United States, and others competed over the spoils of China's lack of internal cohesion. Presciently, Mahan also described China as "being swept irresistibly into the general movement of the world, from which it so long stood apart . . . [and with] a momentous future."[32] Rightly or wrongly, he called China "obstructive by temperament . . . [with] an impulse to overbear its political action by display of force."[33] For another century, being weak, poor, vulnerable, unstable, and introverted, China had none of the prerequisites of being a genuine sea power. Mao called for China to build a powerful navy "to oppose imperialist aggression" and got Soviet help to that end. In reality, sea power was out of the question: If China's economic backwardness made naval strength unrealistic, its economic isolation made naval strength non-essential.

In the 1970s, China's surface fleet grew from 20 to 200 missile-carrying ships, its submarine force grew from 35 to 100 boats, and it developed nuclear-powered submarines. Yet, until 1988, about the time when Deng's strategy went into high gear, China's navy was so

---

32 *Mahan on Naval Strategy*, Hattendorf, 1991, p. 331.

33 *Mahan on Naval Strategy*, Hattendorf, 1991, p. 286.

subordinate to its army that it was led by a PLA general, not an admiral. Though one of the world's largest, its mission was coastal defense, its training was a low priority, and it lacked critical capabilities: naval aviation, anti-submarine warfare, quiet (survivable) open-ocean submarines, and electronic warfare.

A long shift toward sea power began in the mid-1980s and took until the mid-2000s before China embraced sea power as a national, not just naval, priority.[34] This two-decade growth in national awareness, commitment, and capabilities is loosely comparable to the United States from roughly 1880 to 1900, Germany from 1890 to 1914, and Japan from 1920 to 1941. It came about because of the coincidence of the end of the Soviet land threat to China and the commitment of China to trade-based growth. Also, once the Cold War ended, the U.S. naval presence in the Western Pacific, once valued, looked increasingly aimed at China. As China grew and industrialized, it acquired the wherewithal and need to build modern naval and anti-naval capabilities. Again, when a U.S. show of carrier strength foiled their designs in the 1996 Taiwan crisis, Chinese political and military leaders understood that both re-unification and China's overall security interests required the means to prevent the United States from threatening or dictating to China in the region.

This new "major strategic direction" was documented in top-level planning guidance.[35] China's 2004 Defense White Paper "swept aside assumptions regarding land-force preeminence when it stated that the PLA Navy, the PLA Air Force, and the Second Artillery (ballistic missile forces) were to receive priority in funding." China's military priorities were to be "command of the sea, command of the air, and strategic counter-strikes [i.e., nuclear deterrence]."[36]

Now, with China becoming more prosperous, strong, confident, outward-looking, and dependent on oceanic trade, would Mahan recognize it as a sea power? The answer, most likely: not yet. The settlement, or suspension, of China's land-border disputes have permitted

---

[34] McDevitt, 2011.

[35] McDevitt, 2011, pp. 197–204.

[36] People's Republic of China, *China's National Defense in 2004*, white paper, 2004.

significant transfer of resources from ground to naval and anti-naval forces. The PLA Navy (PLAN) has graduated in capabilities and operating range from narrow coastal defense to green and increasingly blue waters.[37] It is now being used to assert Chinese territorial claims and resource rights in the South China and East China Seas, as well as to participate in multinational counter-piracy operations off Somalia's coast. It now regularly practices underway replenishment—a precondition of extending sea power—and has begun to address its deficiencies in naval aviation, quiet submarines, and exploitation of information technology. This last (to be examined at depth in the next chapter) is critical for C4ISR and thus for integrated A2AD operations.

Yet, the Chinese navy's main purpose is still to protect China from U.S. sea-based strike power and potentially a resurgent Japan. Moreover, according a recent study by the Congressional Research Service, it "continues to exhibit limitations or weaknesses in several areas, including capabilities for sustained operations by large formations in distant waters, joint operations with other parts of China's military, C4ISR systems, anti-air warfare, anti-submarine warfare, [and] a dependence on foreign suppliers for certain key ship components."[38] For all the attention China's first aircraft carrier has gotten, it is a refurbished, unimpressive Soviet one. For all the attention its deployment of ships to the Gulf of Aden has gotten, this is the first deployment of Chinese warships outside the Asia-Pacific region since the 15th century and consists of three ships.

Despite the limits of their missions and their reach, China's naval forces appear to be evolving loosely according to the pattern of Germany, the United States, and Japan in the late 19th century: coastal defense of the homeland, then security of territorial waters and shipping approaches, then protection of sea-lanes and commercial interests, then distant power projection. In China's case, holding at risk U.S.

[37] Although the name has been changed by the Chinese to "Chinese Navy," the term PLAN is still widely used and will be used interchangeably with Chinese Navy here.

[38] Ronald O'Rourke, *China Naval Modernization: Implications for U.S. Navy Capabilities—Background and Issues for Congress*, Washington, D.C.: Congressional Research Service, RL33153, October 17, 2012.

carriers within strike range of the mainland was the first priority; now, added emphasis is being placed on backing China's territorial claims and resource interests in the seas around it; Chinese rhetoric and naval investment suggest that China intends not to leave the security of its trade routes, including oil tanker lanes, to others—namely, the U.S. Navy.[39] While the Chinese have not committed to global sea power, their needs and aspirations extend to "far seas," including the entire Pacific and the Indian Ocean.[40]

The debate in China about sea power reveals sophisticated understanding of the issues and challenges involved and, on the whole, is more reassuring than alarming: The hegemonic pattern of 19th- and 20th-century sea powers, per Mahan, is not widely embraced; law-based freedom and rights are stressed; and peaceful use and exploitation of the seas is preferred. Moreover, the Chinese appear to be realistic about both sea control and sea denial. While they seek secure access for trade and resource exploitation, they cannot ignore U.S. sea power, and thus they entertain rules, co-existence, and cooperation. Insofar as they mean to deny others such access, it is to defend China against attack from the sea and to extend security over waters they claim as Chinese. In effect, this outlook fits the regional-global pattern of Chinese interests and strategy identified above: reliance on national strength and, if need be, force, in waters adjacent to China, and willingness to cooperate with the established power beyond those waters.

Even though the Chinese generally buy the economic reasoning that underpinned Mahan's argument for sea power, Chinese thinking about sea power itself is not really Mahanian. He argued that becoming a global power required becoming a global sea power, that commitment to sea power must occupy the entire state and the consciousness of the nation, and that the core capability of a navy is offensive force. Mahan was also clear that a sea power must be able to deny other states, including competing sea powers, secure trade lanes and naval links. To him, sea power was not an extension of territorial defense, regional

39 Ronald O'Rourke, "PLAN Force Structure: Submarines, Ships, and Aircraft," in Saunders et al., eds., 2011, p. 143.

40 O'Rourke, 2011.

hegemony, or cooperation: rather, it was about rivalry and conflict on and for the world's oceans.

Of course, the United States itself was far from a sea power when Mahan wrote *The Influence of Sea Power upon History*. Yet, within 20 years it was strong enough to destroy a Spanish fleet in Manila harbor, convince Great Britain to redirect its sea power elsewhere, and impress the world while circumnavigating it. Production-based economic growth, industrialization, and achievement of continental control enabled the United States to become a sea power; its growing trade, commitment to hemispheric dominance, and determination to be a global power impelled it to do so. China in the early 21st century is similar in some ways: rapidly growing and industrializing; consolidating continental control; heavily dependent on sea trade (much more dependent, in fact, than the United States was in 1890); opposed to foreign naval dominance in its region; and aspiring to be a global power. Yet, even if China evolves in concept and capabilities toward Mahanian sea power, it cannot expect to mount a challenge to American superiority beyond the Western Pacific. The problem for the United States is not Chinese *global sea control*, which is beyond China's grasp, but instead Chinese *regional sea denial*, which is within its grasp.

In the region, Chinese military and political leaders are discovering how useful naval forces are—more so than ground forces—both in protecting the country from the offshore U.S. threats and in pressing Chinese claims in the South China and East China Seas. Including anti-naval capabilities, regional sea power is China's top military priority. Challenging American sea power in the Western Pacific does not require China to develop a large blue-water fleet. As its anti-naval capabilities are increased and improved, making use of advanced information technologies, it is acquiring the means to neutralize U.S. strike power in the region. In time, it could even deny U.S. naval and trade access in a region of great importance to the American economy and, in effect, claim a sphere of influence, similar to what the United States did once it became a hemispheric sea power.

Beyond regional waters, Chinese sea power is but a gleam in the eye: contributing modestly to protection of shipping against Somali pirates, incapable of challenging the United States on the high seas, and effectively relying on the United States to secure trade routes vital for energy supplies and access to world resources and markets. As already noted, the farther from China the Chinese must address security challenges, the more inclined they are to do so cooperatively. As noted, one can see a pattern of Sino-American maritime collaboration in distant regions (e.g., Gulf of Aden) at the same time China threatens U.S. sea power in the Western Pacific.

Based on historical cases of rising powers—the United States, Germany, and Japan—it will be at least two decades before China can apply the skills, doctrine, technology, and logistics to become a global sea power, assuming it decides to do so. However, the crux of the problem for the United States is that China does not need global sea power—i.e., a high-seas fleet—to wield sea power in the Western Pacific with its anti-naval capabilities. China is practicing a form of sea power whereby control, or at least denial, *of* the seas does not necessitate power *upon* the seas. While Mahan did not imagine them, he would be the first to recognize Chinese anti-ship missiles as a feature of sea power no less than the battleships he knew. The challenge to American sea power, and thus American interests, in the Western Pacific is not decades away but looming now. Indeed, China is growing its sea power at a faster pace than the United States is adapting its sea power.

Conclusion: The Interaction of U.S. and Chinese Sea Power

If China means to establish sea denial in East Asian waters, even while enjoying the benefits of U.S. sea power beyond the region, it will be opposed. The United States will not and cannot allow China to deny access to East Asian waters, nor accept a Chinese sphere of influence detrimental to U.S. interests that such sea denial would imply. Yet the Chinese will not—for in their way of thinking they cannot—allow the U.S. Navy to control the Western Pacific without risk or rival. Thus, the analog of Anglo-American accommodation described in the previous chapter breaks down, and that of Anglo-German confrontation seems more applicable. While the United States has not explicitly threatened to sever China's vital trade routes, as it did Japan's in the run-up to Pearl Harbor, opportunities exist for Sino-U.S. sea-power rivalry to become heated and even violent. The United States has the clear ability, possible motivation, and regional encouragement to foil Chinese attempts to use sea power against its neighbors in the South China and East China Seas. It could, if need be, again flaunt its strike power in the event of another Chinese attempt to intimidate Taiwan. Moreover, U.S. planners and pundits could contemplate a blockade of China, e.g., intercepting Chinese shipping in the Malaccan Strait, as a way of bolstering deterrence of Chinese aggression.

For these reasons, it seems highly likely that the Chinese will attempt to neutralize, though not necessarily copy, U.S. sea power in the Western Pacific. Elsewhere, the Chinese will be receptive to cooperative maritime security—their way of reconciling the need for maritime security with the infeasibility of meeting that need unilaterally. They may be satisfied, even pleased, that the United States will continue to secure oil-transport and other shipping routes in the Middle East, across the Indian Ocean, and even through Southeast Asian narrows; for that relieves China of a burden and allows it to concentrate its resources and sea power on challenging its American benefactor-rival in the Western Pacific.

What the United States can and should do, technologically and politically, about the strategic bind it is in is taken up in the next two chapters.

CHAPTER FOUR

Technological Change

> *"Communications dominate war . . . they are the most important single element in strategy, political or military."*
> —A. T. Mahan[1]

The Networking and Targeting Revolutions

Mahan thought and wrote at a time when naval capabilities were limited and operational concepts were defined by the distances of gunnery and visual communications. While he clearly understood the implications of industrialization—from sail to steam and wood to steel—he can be pardoned for believing that the offensive power of the concentrated battle fleet, with the line of dreadnoughts as its spine, was the key to naval victory and world sea power. He died (in December 1914) before the dreadnought proved to be something of a flop—hardly engaged by either side at Jutland (1916).[2] Ironically, the great conflict that Mahan's ideas are blamed for helping to cause began the obsolescence of the very capability that was at the core of those ideas. Whether the ideas themselves transcend technological changes that Mahan and his contemporaries did not contemplate is an important question bearing of the future of sea power and American interests in the Western Pacific.

The technologies for air and undersea warfare that redefined sea power after World War I both were at first resisted by the U.S. Navy. The submarine was described by a young Chester Nimitz as a "Jules

[1] Alfred T. Mahan, *The Problem of Asia and Its Effect upon International Policies*, Boston: Little, Brown and Company, 1900, p. 125, quoted in Hattendorf, 1991.

[2] Irving, 1966.

Verne fantasy" (though Nimitz deserves much of the credit for subsequently developing submarine technology and forces).[3] Although the French and Germans were early leaders in building and using submarines, the Americans—with the Japanese close behind—pioneered the aircraft carrier as the new core of the fleet. By the Battle of Midway, carrier superiority—still concentrated, but at tactical-aircraft range—prevailed, and since then the carrier has been the emblem of sea power. In parallel, electromagnetic-wave technology—radio and radar—extended the ranges of coordinated action and attack. Nuclear power has extended greatly the cruising endurance—not to mention the destructive power—of carriers and submarines.

Just as 19th-century technologies produced and 20th-century technologies soon superseded the sea power observed by Mahan, the information technology is revolutionizing at least the content and perhaps also the concepts of sea power at the beginning of the 21st century. Although the U.S. Navy has pioneered and now stands supreme in exploiting this latest revolution in its capabilities and operating concepts, the effect of these technologies on sea power has only begun. Nowhere is change more evident than in the Western Pacific. And nowhere, because of the interests and capabilities of the established power and the rising power, will change be more consequential.

The information revolution has taken two branches in military affairs in general and naval affairs in particular. Although related in their core technologies, their implications are different enough—in tension, even—that they can be, and here will be, thought of as dual revolutions. The duel of these dual revolutions will affect the course and consequences of sea-power competition for years and probably decades to come. Whether and how the United States will be able to maintain sea power in the Western Pacific despite China's challenge to it depend largely on U.S. technological strategy.

Thanks to digital communications and satellites, computer networking permits forces to be integrated yet also distributed geographically, making them both more effective and less vulnerable. Greater effectiveness comes because any node in the network—any unit, sensor,

---

[3] Borneman, 2012, p. 79.

platform, weapon, or person—located virtually anywhere will be able to work in conjunction with any and every other node.[4] Vulnerability is reduced as enemy forces face greater complexity and expanse in targeting distributed forces. The longer the communications and weapon ranges, the more distributed yet still integrated the whole force can be: Barriers to global communications are being demolished by the creation of information infrastructure, largely for commercial use, and information technology allows weapon ranges to be extended without sacrificing accuracy. In the naval domain, Mahan's insistence on the need to concentrate the fleet to achieve concentrated offensive force has been overtaken by ranges that are theoretically global. Beyond the advantages of being able to connect forces over distance, networking allows those of all services and in all domains—naval, land, air, space, and cyber—to share data and operate jointly, multiplying their effectiveness.

Meanwhile, the information revolution has led to improvements in finding and tracking targets (sensing, for short), in integrating data from diverse sensors (fusing), and in feeding the result to any weapon system (sensor-to-shooter). Also, by guiding weapons from "off-board" navigation systems (e.g., GPS), information technology has reduced the cost of accurate weapons; as a result, a strike force can better afford ample weapons to achieve its missions.[5] When networked with advanced command and control systems, in which human decisionmaking is enhanced by data-crunching and imaging, the result is improved targeting. Technology is making the concentration of naval forces less important than ever even as it is making it more hazardous than ever.

---

[4] This benefit is less pronounced in a hub-and-spoke network than in a node-to-node (any-to-any) network. The former conforms to traditional military command and control systems and largely describes today's status quo. The latter offers unprecedented horizontal integration and flexibility. But it requires sweeping in command and control, which is impeded by institutional resistance and inertia. But it is an aspiration that is permitted by existing technology and will be driven by operational need.

[5] With cheaper and more accurate munitions, the U.S. Air Force and U.S. Navy have had more than enough munitions to carry out their missions in all major campaigns since the Gulf War (Yugoslavia, Iraq, Afghanistan).

Because the purpose of advanced targeting is to weaken or destroy opposing forces, it competes with the networking of those forces, which is intended to make them more survivable. By the same token, the force with the upper hand in *both* networking and targeting can, all else being equal, have a decisive operational edge (assuming its computer networks are not disrupted by cyber-war attacks, an issue to which we will return in short order). At present, U.S. forces hold this dual advantage, especially for "high-intensity" warfare of the sort one might expect with Chinese forces in the Western Pacific.

Although U.S. and Chinese military strategies, requirements, and operating concepts differ, as the preceding chapter explains, both are seeking to make their forces less vulnerable and more effective by advanced networking, while making opposing forces more vulnerable and less effective by advanced targeting. The effects of these technologies on sea power are as pronounced as they are in any military realm. The race between the two countries and between the two revolutions is heating up, and the outcome is not obvious.

U.S. Naval Strengths and Weaknesses

Again, the U.S. military is far ahead of all comers in exploiting information technology. For operations in the Western Pacific, the naval, land, and air forces at the disposal of PACOM can be integrated, regardless of location, through joint C4ISR systems. Sensors available to these forces, whether operated by the U.S. military or by U.S. intelligence services, provide exceedingly fine resolution, wide coverage, and immediacy. Networked, the data from these sensors are fused, analyzed, and shared with forces for targeting their weapons, which have pin-point accuracy. The combined effect is that U.S. strike and expeditionary forces have unmatched speed, reach, and lethality, and thus operational superiority. Because of the ability to call on the whole joint force, every U.S. service is superior in its domain.

The difficulty of taking advantage of these capabilities in actual operations should not be underestimated. People and structures have always been challenged to make the most of revolutionary technologies—think of aviation, submarines, and precision-guided munitions. This takes highly trained personnel, agile command and control, fluid tactics, and seamless inter-service coordination. American sailors, soldiers, and airmen have been learning, practicing, and waging war with these technologies for years now. While problems remain, including a new one in the form of cyber-war, it is fair to say that U.S. forces have as substantial a lead in using information-based capabilities as they do in the technologies embedded in them.

The U.S. Navy has been as energetic as any service in exploiting the dual revolutions. Navies have longed relied on one or another form of networking, which permits specialization in such functions as blockade, sea-lane protection, surface warfare, land bombardment and, in modern times, anti-air warfare (AAW), ballistic-missile defense (BMD), and anti-submarine warfare (ASW). When navies could communicate only at minimal distance and in minimal volume—signal flags, lights, short-range voice radio—coordination required proximity (thus Mahan's principle of concentration). With digital technology and satellites, the range, volume, and speed of naval communications have increased exponentially, making possible a truly networked, and thus more effective and less vulnerable, force. In parallel, greater accuracy at lower cost improves the expected payoff of every weapon used, which multiplies the strike potential of every weapon platform.[6]

The current superiority of the U.S. Navy, in the Western Pacific and globally, is the result not only of its size—which is shrinking—but of the strike potential of each platform, the lethality of each weapon, the power of each sensor, and the integration of all these elements. If the Royal Navy of Mahan's day was more than a match for the next two strongest navies combined, today's networked U.S. Navy has more strike power than all other navies combined.

The problem in the Western Pacific, once again, is not that China is replicating the U.S. Navy but that it is exploiting available technologies to weaken U.S. sea control in the Western Pacific. Despite the U.S. Navy's head start and current advantages, it is not complacent. But

---

[6] This effect was especially striking in the case of aircraft carriers over the past decade or so, which have been able to multiply their effective strike potential without adding aircraft.

institutional change commonly lags technological change, especially when the institution holds a lead over its competitors. While it sees the problem, the Navy is torn between reinforcing the qualities of the existing fleet and developing a very different one. There is a tendency to cling to the familiar in the face of pressures to change. As Lawrence Cavaiola reminds us, Navy brass insisted on putting sails on the USS *Monitor*—just in case!

The U.S. Navy is struggling to keep up with the global demands on it, as well as to retain the upper hand in exploiting information technology vis-à-vis the Chinese. With responsibilities in every region and the cost of ships rising, networking can help make up for limits on the size of the U.S. fleet.[7] In the sea-trading archipelago that is East Asia, the U.S. Navy must secure the oceans, be ready for contingencies from Korea to Taiwan to the South China Sea, and be able to operate in the teeth of improved Chinese targeting. With each ship more capable, all ships networked, and ship-based weapons with greater accuracy and range, American sea power will not be easy for China to dislodge from the region.

At the same time, as previewed in the previous chapter, there is a growing vulnerability in the surface elements of American sea power in the Western Pacific, especially the large aircraft carrier. (Actually, there are two vulnerabilities, the other being the susceptibility of U.S. C4ISR systems to cyber-attack, which we will address later.) Notwithstanding the ability to link and spread forces, the carrier is the greatest concentration of conventional strike-power in naval history—the culmination of Mahanian theory. Even though the range of naval aviation is many times that of naval gunnery, the need to concentrate them in order to concentrate their destructive power persists. During World War II, Admiral "Bull" Halsey insisted, over the objections of Admiral Ernest King, that the carriers operate as a consolidated force against Japanese carriers.[8]

---

[7] For a quantitative analysis of the potential to substitute information for mass, see Stuart Johnson and Arthur Cebrowski, *Alternative Fleet Architecture Design*, Defense and Technology Paper 319, Fort McNair, Washington, D.C.: National Defense University Press, 2005.

[8] Borneman, 2012, p. 210.

If the networking revolution may make the aircraft carrier less essential, the targeting revolution may make it more vulnerable. Despite the superiority of the U.S. Navy, the core of its strike power in the Western Pacific is faced with an increasing risk of being disabled or even destroyed in a major war with China. Insofar as American sea power is equated with carrier power and is crucial for defending U.S. interests and extending U.S. influence, the ability of the United States to prevent Chinese aggression and forestall an East Asian sphere of influence could steadily deteriorate. Yet, because the networking and targeting revolutions are creating alternatives to the carrier, the threat to the carrier does not *necessarily* spell the erosion of American sea power in the Western Pacific. Whether and how these alternatives are pursued may be the most difficult, and uncomfortable, question facing American naval strategists and leaders.

Chinese Priorities, Capabilities, and Potential

Although the U.S. Navy and other U.S. armed services are well ahead of the PLA in exploiting information technology, this is not because of inherent U.S. advantages in science or engineering.[9] Rather, it is because of the U.S. head start. Because of this technology's rapid progress and equally rapid diffusion through global markets, China can be expected to narrow the gap. Moreover, because these technologies are making it easier to deny and harder to control the seas, at least in the Western Pacific, China does not need to match the United States. Technological trends favor targeting over survivability, and thus China over the United States.

Chinese theoretical writings on military exploitation of information technology, which for a while betrayed shallow understanding, are

---

[9] In *Right Makes Might: Freedom and Power in the Information Age* (David C. Gompert, National Defense University Press, 1998), the author makes the case that a free-enterprise system is superior at creating and applying new technology to military purposes. While this tends to advantage democracies, notably the United States, China has managed—so far—to provide free-enterprise conditions without democracy.

now impressive in depth and sophistication.[10] While copying largely accounts for this, copying is a proven path to success in the diffusion of this technology and does not suggest rote or superficiality. Chinese thinking in this realm is now taken very seriously by the U.S. military. For starters, Chinese planners appreciate that the military is a beneficiary of commercial information technology. China has an expanding market share and is increasingly competitive in segments that demand indigenous research and development. Following the East Asian economic-development model, the Chinese started with simple assembly, graduated to micro-components, then made sub-systems, and are now producing complex integrated systems, e.g., high-performance computing, communications, and space systems. For new military systems, the Chinese are curtailing imports from Russia, which is falling behind them in information technology, and instead making their own. Supported by global markets and ballooning revenues, China's information industry is a rising sea that is lifting the PLA. As the Chinese progress in education in science and mathematics and invest their bountiful capital in high-tech, high-value industries, the U.S. commercial edge in information technology will decrease, and the PLA's ability to utilize technology will rival that of the U.S. military.

The Chinese are progressing in virtually all aspects of the networking and targeting revolutions:

- data processing
- digital communications
- full range of sensors (electromagnetic, optical and acoustic)
- sensor fusion
- weapon miniaturization, precision, and range
- space systems for sensing, navigation, and communications
- jamming and counter-jamming
- C4ISR networks
- computer-network attack and exploitation (cyber-war).[11]

---

[10] Andrew S. Erickson and Michael S. Chase, "Information and the Chinese People's Liberation Army Navy," in Saunders et al., eds., 2011, pp. 247–286.

[11] Erickson and Chase, 2011, p. 273.

At the same time, the Chinese know that technologies will not lead to operational improvements, hence not real capabilities, unless matched by investments in the people who use them.[12] Like their American counterparts, they are now emphasizing personnel quality, recruitment, retention, education, and training, not only in technical skills but also in the abilities to use these technologies effectively. China's 2010 Defense White Paper calls for personnel improvements in complex systems, strategic planning, management, standards, policies, maintenance, and joint operations; and it prescribes education best practices, e.g., specialized training commands and distance learning, developed in the West.[13] With China's increasing share in global information technology markets, the PLA has a vast pool of talent from which to draw, though recruitment is a problem (as it has been for the U.S. military). Where the Chinese are deficient, as in high-caliber noncommissioned officers, they know it and mean to redress it.[14]

Like the U.S. Navy, though well behind it, the PLA is developing a "networked fleet," which it intends to integrate into a networked joint force (with PLA air and rocket forces).[15] Their highest priority is to link naval and anti-naval capabilities, including land-based missiles and air power. The missions and reach of this force reflect the evolving Chinese military strategy described in the preceding chapter: from homeland defense to the littoral security to the ability to press Chinese territorial claims to breaking U.S. control of the Western Pacific. China's security perimeter is thus being extended from its coast to the First Island Chain to the Second Island Chain, at least. Initially in this evolution, sensors were of tactical range, communications links were fiber-optical (utilizing inherently more secure land and littoral sea-bed cables), and separate services operated separately. However, as the Chinese extend the range of their targeting into the Pacific, they are stressing space-based sensors, navigation and communications, and jointness.

---

[12] Erickson and Chase, 2011, pp. 259–263.

[13] People's Republic of China, *China's National Defense in 2010*, white paper, 2010.

[14] Erickson and Chase, 2011, p. 262.

[15] Erickson and Chase, 2011, p. 262.

Although the Chinese are applying information technology to solve a host of military-operational challenges, the most critical one is to erect a "kill chain" for the purpose of targeting U.S. forces increasingly far from China:

- Space-based and other extended-range sensors scan larger and larger swaths of the Pacific for U.S. strike platforms, especially carriers.
- Sensor data are fused, processed, analyzed, and disseminated.
- Once found, targets are tracked.
- Command and control systems assign weapons to targets.
- Weapon guidance is enhanced, and costs reduced, by off-board space-based global positioning and navigation systems.
- Weapon lethality is enhanced with terminal homing, including maneuvering warheads.

While it remains to be seen how far into the Pacific the Chinese intend to extend this kill-chain, their immediate goal is to exceed the range of carrier-based strike aircraft, which would also bring forward U.S. air bases in the region into Chinese range. Already, Chinese medium-range ballistic missiles and ground-launched cruise missiles can reach aircraft carriers (and land bases) within 2,000 km of China.[16] The addition of new long-range theater strike systems—a new 4,000 km–range conventional ballistic missile,[17] improved medium-range bombers with long-range cruise missiles,[18] and a growing fleet of quiet attack submarines—will significantly increase the PLA's lethal radius.

---

16 Andrew F. Krepinevich, *Why AirSea Battle?* Washington, D.C.: Center for Strategic and Budgetary Assessments, 2010, p. 24; U.S. Department of Defense, *Military and Security Developments Involving the People's Republic of China*, Annual Report to Congress, 2010, p. 32.

17 Doug Richardson, "China Plans 4,000 Km–Range Conventional Ballistic Missile," *Jane's Missiles and Rockets*, March 1, 2011.

18 Ian Easton, "The Assassin Under the Radar: China's DH-10 Cruise Missile Program," Project 2049 Institute, Futuregram 09-005, 2009.

The PLA's concentration of information technology for anti-naval missions is being complemented by four other priorities:

- ballistic and cruise missile programs that the U.S. Department of Defense describes as "the most active . . . in the world" in numbers and quality[19]
- a modern submarine fleet (see below)
- cyber-war capabilities to degrade U.S. C4ISR networks
- ASAT to destroy satellites on which U.S. C4ISR depend.

Viewed together, the thrust of China's military investment and warfighting strategy is clearly to raise U.S. costs of intervening against China in the event that a regional dispute turns violent. While the original focus was on a Taiwan contingency, the Chinese have generalized their objective.

It is one thing for the PLA to erect a kill-chain and quite another to get it to work as intended. Otherwise, military commanders and political leaders may not have sufficient confidence to act in the face of high costs of failure. Technical and operating skills are essential ingredients, not easily or quickly acquired. PLA enthusiasm over cyber-war and ASAT can be explained in large part by the belief that degrading U.S. C4ISR could compensate for the uncertainties the Chinese face in targeting U.S. strike forces. Even then, the Chinese would have to be confident that two-way cyber and ASAT warfare would be more deleterious to U.S. operations than to their own, given that the United States presumably would respond in kind.

In sum, the Chinese are riding the targeting revolution to disable *U.S. strike platforms*, *U.S. C4ISR* that enables these platforms, and *U.S. satellites* that enable C4ISR. These three U.S. capabilities are at once crucial to U.S. operations and difficult to defend. As Chinese naval and other forces operate throughout the region, the need to distribute and integrate them through networking will also grow. A general pattern in the military-information revolution is that investment and reform, being costly and disruptive, tend to focus on strong operational

---

[19] U.S. Department of Defense, 2010.

demands. For the United States, at present, the priority is to make its forces less vulnerable. For China, it is to make U.S. forces more vulnerable.

Whether in networking or targeting, the Chinese and Americans are both searching for the right approach to command and control: centralized or decentralized. Traditionally, the PLA has stressed centralized-vertical control even more than the U.S. military has. The instantaneous sharing, aggregation, and display of information ("common operating picture" in U.S. defense jargon) can give commanders at the *center* a more complete, accurate, and timely view than they have ever had of what is happening at the fighting *edge*. This can invite excessive meddling and contradict the potency of horizontal collaboration that networking offers. An alternative school argues that networking permits and targeting requires decentralized command and control: sensor-to-shooter integration, initiative at the edge, and the ability to respond to fluid and complex conditions based on latitude to operate within broad guidance. If the Chinese have not resolved the contest between the promise of decentralization and the urge of centralization, they at least understand it.[20] Junior officers tend to better appreciate the pitfalls of centralization than do seniors who are habituated and motivated to take control during hostilities. So the Chinese are likely to gravitate toward decentralization, which will enable them to effectively use new technology to target U.S. forces.

While hard to network because of limits on communications, submarines can also exploit China's improvements in targeting U.S. surface-strike forces at increasing distances from China. The PLAN is replacing an oversized fleet of old, loud, vulnerable coastal-defense submarines with one that, though smaller, is more survivable and capable of operating far from China. Although China can be expected to put more of its strategic-nuclear deterrent force on submarines and also improve anti-submarine submarines, its main mission is anti-carrier warfare. China will deploy nuclear attack submarines as well as advanced, quiet, and relatively cheap diesel submarines. A leading U.S. analyst of both China and sea power describes China's submarines

[20] Erickson and Chase, 2011.

as "the most troublesome problem today" for the U.S. surface fleet in the Western Pacific.[21] Given why the Chinese are developing them, it is expected that these submarines will bristle with anti-surface missiles. Their targets and those of China's anti-ship missiles are the same, which compounds the U.S. vulnerability challenge. This force complements China's commitment to long-range surveillance, sensor fusing, improved tracking, precision navigation and guidance, and integrated C4ISR.[22]

In parallel with deploying submarines and anti-ship missiles, China is building a modern surface fleet. But it is not clear that this will be the workhorse of Chinese sea power in the Western Pacific. Even with a large modern surface fleet, China cannot hope to achieve true sea control in the region, given its vulnerability to multiple U.S. strike capabilities. Nor does China require such a fleet for sea denial—submarines and land-based missiles being more effective, and obviously less vulnerable, for that purpose. Moreover, it would take China decades of investment and experience, as well as creation of an international ring of bases, for the Chinese Navy to rival the U.S. Navy in the blue waters of the Pacific, let alone globally. One must assume that the Chinese will figure out, based on their own progress in targeting over distance, that in the time it would take to build a traditional surface fleet, the survivability of traditional surface fleets will be in doubt.

Rather than trying to replace U.S. sea power with Chinese sea power in the Western Pacific, the Chinese appear to have other purposes in building a surface navy. The first is to complement A2AD capabilities, such as with vessels carrying anti-surface missiles; though vulnerable and thus easier to defeat than submarines and land-based missiles, such vessels add complexity to the threat faced by U.S. naval forces. The second purpose is to enforce Chinese territorial claims in the South China Sea and East China Sea. Provided the United States does not intervene with its naval forces, the Chinese can realistically hope to match Japanese naval power and exceed that of its Southeast Asian neighbors. The third purpose is to join in providing security—

[21] McDevitt, 2011.

[22] O'Rourke, 2011, pp. 141–149.

from pirates, for instance—for its more distant sea-lifelines and chokepoints, such as across the Indian Ocean and in the Strait of Malacca. It can do this unilaterally, multilaterally, or in a tacit division of labor with others (e.g., India and the United States). Fourth, the Chinese understand the value of showing the flag—routinely in peacetime, in response to natural disasters, and in crises—as a way of raising their profile and extending their influence throughout and beyond East Asia.

China's progress in buying or building and deploying aircraft carriers has received much attention in the region and the world. It would take China several decades to build a force of several modern carrier battle groups.[23] Moreover, Chinese aircraft carriers are a poor option for attacking U.S. aircraft carriers, given their limited strike range and their vulnerability. The United States should be thankful if the Chinese were to shift resources from anti-naval capabilities to carriers, which is ironic, given the U.S. attachment to carriers. The Chinese aim to have at most three carriers.[24] Their purposes appear to be like those of the surface fleet as a whole: to influence maritime disputes involving Chinese interests, to contribute to maritime security, and to impress other countries. Because so few countries have them, carriers have a certain great-power aura, though this may fade as their vulnerability becomes acute and apparent.

On the whole, the Chinese have not shown the same commitment to aircraft carriers and other surface naval capabilities as they have to targeting the U.S. fleet. They have several new classes of ships for anti-air and anti-surface missions, but so far they have built only a few ships per class.[25] In addition, China's navy will have a large force of smaller and advanced fast-attack craft armed with missiles; in large numbers, these could present a more serious sea-denial threat than traditional surface combatants.[26] The improvement of amphibious ships has been a high priority: While the obvious mission is in a Taiwan

[23] O'Rourke, 2011, pp. 141–149.

[24] O'Rourke, 2011, p. 150.

[25] O'Rourke, 2011, p. 154.

[26] O'Rourke, 2011, p. 157.

conflict, Chinese writings suggest that landings on other islands may be a desirable option to have.

It could take China decades to build a navy resembling the U.S. Navy—an undertaking the Chinese might well decide is not worth the coin. But China's ambivalence about a traditional high-seas fleet should not gratify the United States, for such a fleet would not be the main challenge to American sea power in the Western Pacific. What matters much more is how well and how soon Chinese forces can carry out the missions assigned to them: anti-access, sea-denial, and bullying China's maritime neighbors. For these purposes, China is progressing rapidly, using targeting technology in which the current sizable U.S. lead will be hard to maintain.

Even with Chinese deployment of new types of missile systems, submarines, and surface vessels, it is their development of an increasingly robust C4ISR network—the central nervous system of A2AD—that represents a qualitatively new and serious challenge to American sea power in the Western Pacific. China is following the U.S. lead in developing and using advanced C4ISR to improve its forces' operational effectiveness. China's 2010 Defense White Paper includes a sophisticated assessment of the PLA's progress in exploiting information technology:

> Significant progress has been made in building information systems for [C4ISR]. Information systems have [also] been widely applied in logistics and equipment support. A *preliminary* level has been achieved in interoperability among command and control systems, combat forces, and support systems, making transmission of orders, intelligence distribution, command, and guidance more efficient and rapid. (emphasis added)

Taking everything into account, the United States should not assume that it has insurmountable advantages in applying information technology to improve the effectiveness and vulnerability of naval or other forces and operations. Technology gaps exist, but they are shrinking as China becomes competitive in today's open and dynamic global IT markets. Gaps in personnel quality, education, and training exist, but the Chinese are making this a high priority. The U.S.

military has a head start in overcoming old-fashioned command and control doctrines and in creating joint C4ISR systems, but the Chinese know what needs to be done. U.S. military "transformation" to networked operations began a decade before China launched its military "informationization" (basically the same thing). But U.S. attention and resources were then diverted to counterterrorism, counterinsurgency, and lengthy military occupations for much of that time. All the while, China's focus has been fixed on neutralizing U.S. sea power in the Western Pacific. Moreover, the United States is currently dependent on the concentration of strike power in a few large aircraft carriers, whereas China is stressing capabilities that exploit the networking and targeting revolutions.

Implications of Current Trends

U.S. attempts to defend carriers, regional bases, and other strike platforms against Chinese ballistic missiles face a daunting numbers problem: For the same amount of resources, China can add more deliverable missiles to its arsenal than the United States can expand its ability to intercept them.[27] In addition, China's cyber-war and ASAT capabilities are, according to PLA writings, intended to disrupt U.S. C4ISR and thus deter, delay, degrade, or defeat U.S. intervention in the Western Pacific.[28]

If current trends continue, U.S. naval and other forces will be at risk from Northeast to Southeast Asia—e.g., in a confrontation with China over North Korea's collapse or a crisis in the South China Sea. Such deterioration of the survivability of the U.S. surface fleet has implications at several levels. The PLA is more able to degrade, delay, defeat, or deter U.S. intervention and to prevent U.S. strikes on China.

---

27 The advantage of missile delivery over missile intercept is the function of several factors among them: the higher cost of interceptors, when taking targeting systems into account; the feasibility of penetration aids (e.g., decoys); the introduction of multiple independently targetable re-entry vehicles (MIRVs); and the cost of expanding sea-based or land-based interceptor launch installations.

28 See Gompert and Saunders, 2011.

With U.S. intervention less likely to succeed or even to occur, China improves its odds of prevailing in conflicts with local states over territory or resources, and thus is in a stronger position to prevail through coercion. If the United States responds by pulling forces out of the PLA's growing range, those forces would be more survivable but less able to intervene or to influence events in the region. The option of keeping surface forces forward in peacetime and steaming them out of harm's way in the event of a heightened Chinese threat would obviously undermine U.S. leverage in a crisis.

Whether U.S. naval forces in the Western Pacific are withdrawn beyond China's anti-naval radius or instead remain and become more vulnerable, China's neighbors, including long-standing U.S. allies, will be more exposed, less confident, and perhaps more likely to yield Chinese pressure to the disadvantage of U.S. interests. Such developments could in time amount to Chinese sea denial and hegemonic sphere of influence, as defined earlier, in the Western Pacific. Alternatively, it could lead to a breakdown of the order and peace that this vital region has enjoyed for half a century. These are the very outcomes that U.S. sea power in the Western Pacific is meant to prevent.

Even if the Chinese do not harbor hegemonic ambitions, their interests, as explained above, will almost certainly lead them to continue efforts that could have these effects. At a minimum, China's territorial defense—an imperative on which there is not disagreement in China—compels it to push U.S. carriers beyond the strike range of China. It is unrealistic to think that China will tolerate the nearness of forces that are able and, in the event of war, meant, to attack China, now that China can challenge that presence. Beyond homeland defense, the Chinese wish to have the upper hand in resolution of regional disputes involving Chinese territorial claims (Taiwan and the South China Sea) or national security (Korea), and to dislodge the United States as the preeminent security provider in the region. The United States can only assume that the challenge to its sea power in the Western Pacific will grow as China gets stronger.

The problem of gaining and keeping access to a distant region is inherently harder than that of denying such access by a highly capable state of the region. Investments in long-range sensors, missiles, and submarines and in the people to operate them will yield increasing returns for China, whereas remaining invested in traditional strike forces will yield diminishing returns for U.S. interests. Pressure is mounting on the United States to switch to another investment strategy.

U.S. Responses

American strategists may believe that some native technological superiority will enable the United States to prevail in its sea-power contest with China in the Western Pacific. This is a delusion, given China's increasing competitiveness and the efficiency with which these technologies spread throughout their global market. Rather, a new U.S. advantage will have to come from being smarter in using information technology—smarter than it has been, and smarter than the PLA.

Both geographic and technological asymmetries tend to favor China over the United States. The United States needs to be able to project power to a region 10,000 miles away, whereas China needs to be able to thwart U.S. power projection to its own region. In addition, the reach and quality of Chinese targeting can improve *by degree*, whereas the United States must shift *in kind* because of the vulnerability of its existing strike platforms. The sorts of capabilities the Chinese need to target U.S. sea power and impede U.S. power projection exist and are improving linearly, and rapidly. In contrast, the surface vessels on which the United States currently relies predate the information revolution. While their *effectiveness* is being enhanced with information technology, their *vulnerability* is a consequence of being slow, few, visible, and of restricted strike range—physical traits that technology cannot remove. Thus, if both China and the United States proceed with incremental advances at current levels of investment, China's targeting will outpace U.S. efforts to maintain survivable strike power.

This is not to say that the U.S. Navy is not seized with the problem. In league with the U.S. Air Force, its Air-Sea Battle strategy, mentioned earlier, is a serious effort to counter the A2AD problem—

globally, but with China and the Western Pacific foremost in mind.[29] As an integrated approach, Air-Sea Battle is analogous to the Air-Land Battle approach organized by the Army and Air Force in the 1980s to counter the Soviet armored threat to NATO. The United States and its European allies had concluded that neither static forward defense nor nuclear escalation was an acceptable solution to that threat. As an alternative, Air-Land Battle called for better communications and closer collaboration between the Army and Air Force, not only in operations but also in modernization. But there was more to it than that—namely, deep attack. Air-Land Battle exploited U.S. advances in surveillance and advantages in precision weapons, cruise missiles, and stealth to strike beyond the Soviet front line of assault. Instead of beefing up static forward defense or resorting to nuclear weapons, NATO could attack deeper echelons of Soviet combat forces and support, thus weakening the entire assault. Against new forms of U.S. air power, the Soviets had no good defense and thus no real answer.

Air-Sea Battle is fundamentally like Air-Land Battle in that it responds to the declining viability of forward defense in combination with growing aversion to strategic escalation. But it is far more advanced because it exploits the network and targeting revolutions. Thanks to digital communications, the possibility for integrated operations is much greater now, as is the ability to strike with greater precision at greater range. But there is more to Air-Sea Battle than integration: Like its ancestor, it is essentially designed for deep attack against enemy forces and support systems. Moreover, such attacks can be carried out by both kinetic and cyber weapons on everything from physical forces and sensors to the computer networks that enable them.

Operationally, Air-Sea Battle will present the Chinese with serious problems. However, the question lingers: Does it solve the vulnerability problem, and thus the deterioration of American sea power in the Western Pacific? The answer is unclear. Insofar as it depends on few, forward, slow, or stationary concentrations of strike power—carriers

---

[29] Norton A. Schwartz (Gen., USAF) and Jonathan W. Greenert (Adm., USN), "AirSea Battle: Promoting Stability in an Era of Uncertainty," *The American Interest*, February 20, 2012.

and bases in the region—Air-Sea Battle is a modest improvement in the face of a challenge that requires an immodest one. In the fuller technological and geo-strategic context, Air-Sea Battle may be necessary, but it is not sufficient.

The other strategic issue raised by Air-Sea Battle is whether it makes the United States more dependent on military preemption or escalation than it ought to be. The time to strike Chinese target and strike capabilities is before they are used to disable U.S. forces. This creates a strong urge for the United States to attack earlier than it would otherwise choose. Moreover, Air-Sea Battle is potentially destabilizing in that the Chinese would have an incentive to attack before their capabilities to do so are reduced by U.S. preemption. In addition, because many elements of the Chinese kill-chain are located in China, attacking them would be escalatory. To be clear, the United States should not rule out attacking Chinese mainland capabilities that can be used against it, and the threat to do so can strengthen deterrence. But having escalatory options is very different, strategically and politically, than becoming dependent on them—or on preemption—for lack of alternatives.

Even with Navy–Air Force integration and options to strike early and deep against Chinese A2AD capabilities, the United States must rely increasingly on more distant and/or less observable platforms as the survivability of its forward forces declines. How radically this shift occurs is one of the most important questions facing the U.S. military, especially the U.S. Navy.[30] Unless the vulnerability problem is solved, pressures will mount to place more emphasis in U.S. military strategy toward China on deterrence based on the threat of escalation. Yet, as noted earlier, the United States will not want to rely on the threat to resort to nuclear weapons at a time when it is trying to de-emphasize the role of these weapons in warfare. Moreover, China will certainly have a second-strike nuclear deterrent force capable of riding out a U.S. first strike and overwhelming U.S. missile defense. U.S. options

[30] The Air Force already has long-range, including global, strike options and is pursuing others.

to escalate to strategic cyber-attacks or use of ASAT will also become more risky and less credible as China develops such capabilities.[31]

Some forward basing and operations in the Western Pacific, though vulnerable, will remain necessary in order to support the capabilities of local allies, raise the bar against the use of force, and increase the credibility of security guarantees. Moreover, the traditional role of forward presence in reassuring friends, demonstrating commitment, and influencing peacetime developments will not vanish. But with both forward defense and escalation getting riskier, the United States will need to use technology more inventively.

A New Posture in the Pacific: Toward Phantom Sea Power

There are four ways to counter advanced targeting:

- Defend the target.
- Disable the capabilities that can strike the target.
- Hide the target.
- Complicate the target.

The first of these is a natural military reflex and heretofore the default option. However, given foreseeable technology, it may be the least fruitful. Both submarine warfare and missile warfare, two of China's highest priorities, are offense-dominant in that returns on additional investment in offensive capabilities exceed returns on equivalent investment in defenses against those capabilities. In both realms, defense is technologically difficult, operationally undependable, and economically dear. For all the investment in ballistic missile defense (BMD) in the last quarter-century, it is still—and likely to remain—inadequate or prohibitively expensive against large and sophisticated attacks by large and sophisticated states.[32] Current ("hit-to-kill") BMD may work and be worth the cost against the likes of Iran and North Korea, but

---

31 See Gompert and Saunders, 2011.

32 See Gompert and Saunders, 2011.

not China, which can multiply and improve the penetrability of its missiles more readily than the United States can increase its missile-intercept capacity. Perhaps directed-energy or other exotic technologies will be able to achieve meaningful levels of success against large attacks/attackers, but do not count on it.

Despite having been vigorously pursued much longer than BMD has, anti-submarine warfare (ASW) remains frustrating: Submarines are simply very hard to find. Deep waters with distinct thermal layers are sanctuaries to quiet, hiding vessels. Because acoustic listening (passive sonar) can usually be defeated by silencing submarine machinery, non-acoustic technology received a lot of attention during the Cold War and since; but the results have disappointed. Moreover, sinking or disabling hard-to-locate submarines with conventional (non-nuclear) weapons is problematic. The lesson China has taken from the discouraging history of ASW is that it makes sense to invest in a new submarine force, even against the world's best (U.S.) ASW. Presumably, the U.S. Navy and U.S. Strategic Command believe that submarines are not about to become detectable and vulnerable, or they would not place the increasing reliance they do on that leg of the strategic nuclear triad.

As noted, given the difficulty and cost of defending U.S. strike platforms in the Western Pacific, American military strategists are turning to the idea of counter-targeting Chinese sensors, land- and sea-based missile-launchers, command and control centers, weapon stocks, air bases, and submarine bases. The technological possibilities and strategic risks associated with Air-Sea Battle have already been covered and need not be repeated. What deserves more discussion is the option of attacking the Chinese kill-chain with cyber weapons. While the United States and its armed forces have yet to develop a doctrine for cyber-war, including whether or not to initiate it, they are trending toward making it an element of their war-fighting capabilities and plans.

The Chinese have identified C4ISR networks as PACOM's Achilles' Heel and fair game for cyber-attack; so it is not as if the United States would be triggering cyber-war that would not occur if it abstained from attacking Chinese C4ISR. As the Chinese have identified U.S. C4ISR as the greatest vulnerability of U.S. capabilities and plans, so will China's C4ISR vulnerability grow as it extends the reach of its sensors, weapons, and communications far beyond China's coast. Conversely, if the Chinese do not increase the geographic reach of their C4ISR capability, they cede the vastness of the Pacific to U.S. strike forces. The Chinese have to balance the increased risks associated with extended anti-naval capability against the increased risks of not extending that capability. So far, it appears that the Chinese are determined to extend their reach, which in turn presents the United States with an opportunity to counter it.

Cyber-war is generally regarded as an off-shoot of the military information revolution. However, because its targets are enemy targeting and networking, cyber-war is better thought of as a military information *counter*-revolution. If a force becomes operationally and technically dependent on advanced networking and targeting, cyber-war has the potential to place it at a severe disadvantage. The U.S. and Chinese militaries are both increasingly dependent yet are also two of the world's most capable cyber-war states. Both forces have much to lose as well as to gain from cyber-war, given that it is also offense-dominant. Obviously, the side that is better at cyber-war and also at operating despite degradation from cyber-war would have the advantage. But it is not easy to figure which side that would be. One could imagine the United States being superior to China at cyber-war yet inherently more vulnerable to degradation in the event of cyber-war, given the geographic distance it must cover and its reliance on advanced C4ISR.

As a way of enhancing survivability of U.S. forces in the Western Pacific, offensive cyber-war against the central nervous system of China's anti-access capability would, in effect, be defensive. Firewalls, patching, and other network-security measures can provide essential, if imperfect, protection against lesser state and non-state cyber threats. But against projected offensive cyber-war capabilities and complex attacks on the United States—and on China—defense will prove inadequate.[33] Because much IT infrastructure is dual-use, civil-military cyber-attacks against enemy C4ISR systems run a serious danger of

---

[33] See Gompert and Saunders, 2011.

escalation to general cyber-war, including against dual-purpose networks, critical cyber infrastructure, commercial, and civilian systems. Given their network vulnerabilities, the difficulty of defense, and the other side's offensive strength, both the United States and China will have strong aversions to such escalation. This presents a major dilemma—the likelihood of cyber-war against C4ISR in the event of Sino-U.S. conflict versus the severe consequences of general cyber-war—that can only be resolved by the exercise of tight political control by both states to avert escalation.[34]

In the final analysis, the United States will be torn between conducting cyber-war to help protect its military forces in the Western Pacific and avoiding cyber-war because of the growing reliance of those same forces on networking. Moreover, given the possibility and consequences of cyber-war escalating and spreading once begun—crashing networks of national importance along the way—the United States will have a strong interest in mutual restraint. Yet it is quite possible that the Chinese would not show restraint even if the United States did, which argues for the United States at least being prepared technically and doctrinally to wage cyber-war in the event of armed conflict.[35] U.S. military and civilian planners have not yet sorted out what role cyber-war could play in a major armed conflict. Meanwhile, the U.S. military cannot be expected to refrain from acquiring capabilities and making plans to degrade Chinese forces that are meant to attack U.S. forces. As the latest U.S. national defense strategy and Air-Sea Battle both suggest, cyber-war is increasingly viewed as an integral part of U.S. assumptions and plans.[36]

Similar dynamics and dilemmas are at work in regard to military use of space and ASAT. U.S. C4ISR relies vitally on communications, surveillance, and positioning satellites for operations in the expansive

---

[34] See Gompert and Saunders, 2011.

[35] Gompert and Saunders (2011) report on Chinese military writings that stress the advantages of initiating cyber-war as a way of blinding U.S. C4ISR—i.e., not for deterring U.S. cyber attacks. Some of this writing indicates advantages for China to initiate early and even preemptively.

[36] See Schwartz and Greenert, 2012.

Western Pacific. Chinese reliance on satellites for the same purposes will grow as its C4ISR reaches outward. Both are likely to have both hard- and soft-kill ASAT. But in space, more than in cyber-space, there is a possibility of mutual deterrence and restraint. At present, the United States has essentially recognized that it has more to lose than to gain in ASAT war.[37]

U.S. misgivings about crossing the ASAT and cyber-war thresholds in a conflict with China should be tempered by the likelihood that the Chinese themselves would not hesitate to cross these thresholds early in, or even as a precursor to, hostilities. Still, the vital reliance of U.S. forces, not to mention the nation as a whole, on the use of space and cyber-space suggests that the United States, as a matter of strategy and policy, would not want to become *dependent* on these new forms of warfare to prevail in a conflict with China and to preserve American power in the Western Pacific.

The option of hiding U.S. platforms from Chinese targeting may be more feasible and affordable than defending them and more prudent than relying on preemptive or escalatory strikes (à la Air-Sea Battle, cyber-war, and ASAT). Platforms can be hidden simply by keeping them beyond the reach of enemy sensors. Yet, their own weapons must still be able to reach their targets. This excludes the solution of keeping large U.S. aircraft carriers beyond Chinese targeting distance, which will exceed that of the strike range of carrier-based manned aircraft. While there is probably a role for U.S. surface-based long-range missiles in response to Chinese A2AD capabilities, it is a matter of time and money—the Chinese have both—before China is able to deploy constellations of space-based sensors that can scan beyond the Western Pacific. If the U.S. Navy aspires to achieve what it has coined "global maritime awareness" (relying on contributions from other U.S. military and intelligence satellites), China has the wherewithal to deploy such capabilities within the time-frame of this analysis. China is a growing space power, with plans to launch 10 satellites on average per year, com-

---

[37] U.S. space policy refers to access to space as "vital" and implies that ASAT is mainly for deterrence. See for example Gregory Schulte, DoD, testimony to Congress, May 2010.

pared with 17 for the United States.[38] As for missiles, the Chinese are already able to achieve long range (albeit for nuclear, not conventional missions), the accuracy of which can be enhanced by space-based geo-positioning technology.

A corollary of U.S. faith in ballistic missile submarines is that submarines make very survivable conventional-strike platforms because Chinese ASW, even as it improves, has little chance of finding them. The U.S. Navy is already increasing the role of submarines for precision strike with conventional ballistic and cruise missiles. How many and what kind of submarines should be made available for this purpose remain important open questions. The way the United States designs and builds submarines—especially nuclear-powered ones—is very expensive. The U.S. commitment to nuclear submarines reflects the need for distant and lengthy patrolling. Yet, large numbers of much cheaper and quiet non-nuclear submarines—even with shorter "legs"—must be a serious U.S. conventional-strike option for the U.S. Navy as China improves and extends its anti-surface capabilities.

Hand in hand with hiding U.S. targets is befuddling Chinese targeting systems and the people who use them by presenting increased complexity. For the U.S. Navy, more numerous, diverse, small, fast, and stealthy strike platforms (and decoys) would be a major challenge for a Chinese targeting system that is designed against a few, big, slow,

---

[38] One expert described the military impact of Chinese space capabilities in these terms:

> Increasingly sophisticated space based systems expand PLA battle-space awareness and support extended range conventional precision strike systems. Space assets enable the monitoring of naval activities in surrounding waters and the tracking of air force deployments into the region. The PLA is investing in a diverse set of increasingly sophisticated electro-optical (EO), synthetic aperture radar (SAR), and electronic reconnaissance assets. Space-based remote sensing systems also provide the imagery necessary for mission planning functions, including automated target recognition technology that correlates preloaded optical, radar, or infrared images on a missile system's computer with real time images acquired in flight. A constellation of small electronic reconnaissance satellites, operating in tandem with SAR satellites, could provide commanders with precise and timely geo-location data on mobile targets. Satellite communications also offer a survivable means of linking sensors to strike systems, and will become particularly relevant as PLA interests expand further from PRC borders. (Mark A. Stokes, Prepared Statement for U.S.-China Economic and Security Review Commission hearing on the Implications of China's Military and Civil Space Programs, May 11, 2011)

and unmistakable high-value ones. Drones—surface and sub-surface vessels and ship-launched aircraft—are less costly and more expendable, obviously, than manned systems. In larger numbers, and in combination with diverse strike platforms, they can complicate Chinese targeting and C4ISR, not to mention air defense. Because a diverse alternative force could be widely distributed, instead of concentrated like large carriers, the surveillance and tracking problem alone would be much more difficult.

Aircraft carriers could have a place in a posture aimed at complicating Chinese targeting—but not necessarily huge ones carrying manned aircraft and affordable in very small numbers. With the performance of drones climbing, their cost dropping, and eventually their size shrinking, aircraft carriers can be smaller, cheaper, diverse, and numerous. To invoke a tenet of sea power, numbers matter—even against large missile forces. To illustrate *simply*, imagine two alternative naval strike forces of equal strike power: one made up of a few large strike platforms (e.g., today's aircraft carriers) and the other of many small ones (e.g., tomorrow's drone carriers). Then say it is no harder for enemy sensors to target a given large strike platform than a given small one and, further, that it takes twice as many enemy missiles to destroy a large platform as it does a small one. If the number of strike platforms in the large-platform force is less than half the number of strike platforms in the small-platform force, more strike power will survive a missile attack of a given size on the latter than the former.[39]

The advantages of proliferating naval strike platforms can be found in an analysis by researchers at the U.S. National Defense University in 2005.[40] That work evaluated quantitatively the expected operational performance against a large adversary of four options: the U.S. Navy's programmed strike force and three alternative strike forces *of equal cost* with larger numbers of smaller platforms. All three

---

[39] While this illustration is merely arithmetic, its assumptions are, if anything, conservative given current technological possibilities. For example, small, diverse, scattered strike platforms—not to mention submerged ones—could each be harder to find and hit than large conspicuous ones.

[40] Johnson and Cebrowski, 2005.

alternatives relied heavily on vertical and short take-off-and-landing (VSTOL) aircraft; and one was especially ambitious in making use of drones. All three relied more on submarines and on unmanned platforms of all sorts. The total number of strike platforms ranged from about 200 in the programmed fleet to about 800 in the most radical alternative. The analysis of expected results showed that all three alternatives were capable of 25–50 percent greater strike effectiveness than the programmed fleet, when taking into account losses from enemy attacks. The most effective force was the one that differs most from the current fleet. True, this alternative was a revolutionary departure from the traditional naval force. But that's the whole point: The networking and targeting branches of the information revolution are already well underway.[41] A revolution in structures and platforms should follow. At the same time, the requisite technologies for the alternative fleet architectures already exist.

The National Defense University study recommends four design principles for future naval forces:

- complexity—large numbers of diverse, fast, agile, low-signature, ambiguous, diverse platforms
- smaller ships—taking advantage of improvements in strike-payload thanks to better weapons accuracy
- networking—across large areas for the enemy to search, track, and target
- modularity—permitting diverse platforms based on a few simple hull types.

In addition to significant operational advantages, the alternative fleet architectures, being of equal cost, would largely solve the problem of the Navy having too few ships to cover too much ocean and too many missions. (Why the U.S. Navy has not embraced these and other innovative ideas will be taken up shortly.)

Overall, without discarding concepts to degrade Chinese A2AD capabilities, the most feasible, affordable, and prudent U.S. ways to counter China's targeting advances are to hide, fractionate, diversify,

---

[41] Johnson and Cebrowski, 2005.

and otherwise complicate the target set—U.S. strike platforms. These approaches, taken together, would present the Chinese with a vexatious and qualitatively different problem than the one they are now working so hard to solve. They would present the Chinese with the opposite of the concentration of offensive forces that was the heart of Mahanian sea power. Chinese sensors would reveal not a few large and unmistakable "blips" but rather hazy, cluttered, ambiguous, and unstable screens (if not darkened ones). By more fully exploiting networking technology than it does now, the United States could distribute *forces* while still being able to concentrate *force*. This, after all, was what Mahan was driving at—the ability to gain dominance in war, and preponderance in peace, by superior concentration of force—only the technology of the time suggested no way other than to concentrate the surface battle fleet. After his initial shock, Mahan would approve. After all, he was the one to explain that sea power was power *of* the sea; he just assumed that this required power *on* the sea.

We might call this combination confounding enemy targeting "phantom sea power": far less vulnerable yet no less capable of coordinated and concentrated strikes; a new way to exercise sea denial and to mitigate enemy sea denial; using the networking revolution to trump—at least for now—the targeting revolution. A more survivable U.S. strike posture along these lines would be neither escalatory nor destabilizing; rather, it would discourage Chinese preemptive attack, obviate the need for U.S. preemptive attack, and allow time for a crisis to be defused.

The practical elements of phantom sea power would include:

- submarines
- sea-based missiles of various ranges
- drone vessels and aircraft, in large numbers
- larger numbers of small vessels with drones and missiles
- state-of-the-art and continuously improving C4ISR networks
- cyber-war[42]
- ASAT.[43]

---

[42] While recognizing the strategic risks of actual use.

[43] Again, while recognizing the strategic risks of actual use.

This is not to say that legacy platforms, including large aircraft carriers, have no future in the Western Pacific. The traditional blue-water fleet will remain potent, relevant, and survivable in most regions, and thus will be available for East Asia. Carriers and other surface combatants may have important roles to play in conditions short of high-intensity Sino-U.S. warfare, which is among the least likely contingencies. Moreover, as we will see, surface combatants will remain important in expressing U.S. commitment and advancing U.S. interests—roles for which more ethereal war-fighting capabilities, as prescribed here, are not suitable. At issue is the balance between concentrated, conspicuous sea power and spread-out, ghost-like sea power. The analysis here suggests that the balance should tilt increasingly and as soon as practical toward the latter.

Even if a survivable posture such as the one described here can restore and maintain U.S. operational advantages and sea power in the Western Pacific, important questions remain:

- Can this survivable posture be sustained against further Chinese research, development, and investment in advanced capabilities?
- How vulnerable will it be to cyber-war?
- Will the U.S. Navy take this direction?

Again, the Chinese have chosen to concentrate on denying U.S. sea control in the Western Pacific instead of achieving sea control for themselves. Will the Chinese approach succeed if the United States shifts toward phantom sea power? On the surface (no pun intended), it would be much harder for the Chinese to neutralize a force of U.S. submarines, drones, and numerous, distant, and diverse strike platforms because they will not be able to find and target enough of them. Eventually, breakthroughs in sensor technology may make any platform, anywhere, observable and vulnerable. Until then, the fragmentation, distribution, diversification, and hiding of strike forces will cause diminishing returns on investment in targeting.

As great a risk to distributed U.S. sea power as Chinese targeting is Chinese cyber-warfare. In theory, cyber-warfare has the potential to disrupt all kinds of military operations that exploit information technology. How great the potential and what can be done about it over the long term is unclear. It may be that progress in defending computer networks from low-end threats (e.g., hackers) will extend to high-end ones (e.g., China). In the meantime, the United States will have to grapple with the dilemma of how dependent to become on networking—but so too will China.

Implementation: Need Versus Inertia

The U.S. Navy is not poised to embark on a radical shift away from concentrated surface power. Large carriers have the backing of naval and joint commanders, diplomats, politicians, and ship-builders. Moreover, but for their vulnerability to Chinese targeting, they remain critical to U.S. global military and political power. If the number of U.S. carriers declines, it will be gradually, carefully, and by attrition through retirement from old age. Within the likely constraints of U.S. defense spending, the retention of aircraft carriers—at about $10 billion per vessel—will limit the building of distributed sea power to investments at the margin. Hence, it will take the United States decades to effect wholesale change in the character and composition of its fleet.

In addition to huge industrial and structural impediments, navies—especially those of established sea powers—resist rapid change. For instance, the Royal Navy was very slow to change from sail to steam and wood to steel until compelled to do so by emergent German sea power. An even more arresting example is the case of the battleship following World War I. The advent of submarines and warplanes and the marginal role played by the dreadnought in the war, despite expectations that it would be critical, raised questions—*outside* the U.S. Navy's mainstream—about both the survivability and importance of battleships. In 1920, Brigadier General Billy Mitchell of the Army Air Service challenged the Navy to see whether its battleships could withstand bombing. The Navy insisted on "the improbability of a modern battleship being either destroyed or completely put out of action by aerial bombs."[44] It further asserted that "no development would justify any conclusion that battleships were practically rendered useless by aircraft."[45] Mitchell's bombers proceeded to sink the Navy's captured German battleship *Ostfriesland* with six bombs in 20 minutes.[46] From then on, the vulnerability of the battle ship was indisputable, its demise was inevitable, and the supremacy of the aircraft carrier was assured. While it took the Navy another 20 years to accept the battleship's obsolescence, it finally stopped building them in 1944, a year in which it built six aircraft carriers.

Now imagine a new rendition of old Navy assurances of the invincibility of the battleship, substituting aircraft carrier for battleship and long-range anti-ship ballistic missile for aerial bomb. It is hard to think of a persuasive reason why aircraft carriers can defy technological progress when battleships could not. Yet the Navy's defense of aircraft carriers echoes its defense of battleships when they had become vulnerable. Moreover, because the aircraft carrier will continue for years to play an essential role in U.S. strategy and operations *globally*, it is not easy to shift toward a different posture for one region, however important, because of a particular problem there, however acute. Global sea powers tend to have global navies.

The U.S. Navy, like all big navies, needs a long time to change, given how long it takes to design and build new ships and the aversion to mothballing serviceable and hugely expensive existing platforms. But this is all the more reason to start changing now. The danger is that surface fleets will obsolesce gradually, as the targeting revolution spreads, with nothing fundamental being done about it. Whether because of institutional caution or long lifetimes of ships, the U.S. Navy's structure is very slow to change. This can be illustrated by the percentages of total fleet composed of submarines, aircraft carriers, and other surface combatants over the past half-century (putting aside what the optimal percentages should be), shown in Table 2.

---

44 William Leahy, quoted in Borneman, 2012, p. 105.

45 Secretary of the Navy Josephus Daniels, quoted in Borneman, 2012, p. 105.

46 So confident was Mitchell that he declined to conduct the test against the old USS *Iowa*, as the (equally confident) Navy had offered.

Table 2
U.S. Navy Structure, 1960–2010 (percentage of total)

Year	Submarines	Aircraft Carriers	Surface Combatants
1960	14%	3%	34%
1970	14%	3%	34%
1980	16%	3%	34%
1990	17%	2%	35%
2000	17%	3%	38%
2010	18%	3%	42%

SOURCE: Naval History and Heritage Command website, no date.

Since 1960, there has been a lot of modernization but practically no change in the structure of the U.S. fleet. Requirements have changed radically from early in the Cold War until now; but fleet composition has not budged, even with the disappearance of the rival superpower. Moreover, despite the growing threat to surface warships, their share of the total fleet has actually increased.

As another illustration, the United States commissioned 10 battleships from 1941 to 1944, 20 years after their vulnerability to aerial bombing was demonstrated. Of these, some were scrapped a few years later, some were turned into memorials, and some were retired and returned to brief service years later. "By the time the Iowa-class giants [battleships] slid down the ways, the aircraft carrier had established its dominance as the navy's principal capital ship."[47] While there are many factors that explain such rigid ratios and anomalies, the fact remains that the U.S. Navy changes its structure at a nearly imperceptible pace, despite changes, often dramatic, in the world around it. The significance of these observations is that improvements in anti-naval capabilities require an ability to change that is uncharacteristic of established sea powers and their navies.

---

[47] Borneman, 2012, p. 486.

The problem, of course, is that progress in Chinese targeting of the U.S. fleet can be significant in years, not decades. While it would take much longer for China to become a traditional high-seas power—as it took the United States, Japan, and Germany roughly 20 years—the pace at which the Chinese are applying the technology, skills, and operating concepts to threaten U.S. sea power in the Western Pacific is faster. As a result, even if the U.S. Navy were now to move with uncharacteristic speed in the direction proposed here, American sea power in the Western Pacific will come under pressure at a critical time in Sino-U.S., East Asian, and world affairs.

Conclusions

In sum, current technological trends affecting sea power in the Western Pacific are unfavorable to the United States. Chinese targeting capabilities are progressing more rapidly than U.S. responses. While the United States remains generally superior in its mastery of information technology for both commercial and military uses, the Sino-U.S. gap has been shrinking and will keep shrinking. In applying this technology, the Chinese have an easier problem to solve in targeting U.S. forces than the United States has in trying to stem the growing vulnerability of its surface fleet. Moreover, the core of U.S. sea power, the large carrier, does not exploit the networking revolution and may be a casualty of the targeting revolution.

While China can further its targeting advantages through steady enhancements, the United States must make a big move to render Chinese targeting ineffective: toward distributed, diverse, and elusive strike forces of submarines, drones, and small surface platforms. Air-Sea Battle can help by providing counter-targeting; but it could be destabilizing, and it does not fundamentally solve the problem of the vulnerability of surface ships, on which U.S. strike power depends.

Even then, if the U.S. Navy decided soon on its next big move, implementation would take decades, especially since surface forces are still useful and survivable in the rest of the world. At best, being realistic, the Navy will gradually shift from a vulnerable to a survivable strike posture in the Pacific—much slower than Chinese anti-surface improvements. Meanwhile, cyber-war—at which both the United States and China are gaining proficiency—will work more to the operational disadvantage of the United States than of China, though this will become more balanced as the Chinese come to rely more on C4ISR for long-range targeting and coordination of more distributed forces. Moreover, targeting capabilities may eventually progress to the point that even more distributed, diverse, and numerous U.S. strike platforms will become vulnerable. Thus, technology does not offer the United States a permanent way out of its Western Pacific predicament.

Whatever the long term holds, the near-to-medium term could be especially critical for the United States. As Sino-American relations and East Asian affairs enter a period of heightened uncertainty, Chinese operational-military advantages could unsettle Japan and other important regional states, encourage Chinese risk-taking, and create the appearance, at least, that the expansion of Chinese power comes at the expense of the United States.

Once again, East Asia is too important for U.S. interests to allow it to become a Chinese sphere of influence by withdrawing U.S. power or leaving it vulnerable. This raises the question of whether there are "political" solutions to the problem of the entanglement of U.S. and Chinese sea power in a region vital to both. For that, we need to revisit our historical cases and also analyze the effects, challenges, and opportunities presented by the convergence of Chinese and U.S. interests in maritime security as a consequence of globalization.

A final note about the impact of technology: It may be that the information revolution, especially the targeting revolution as it plays out at sea, will make sea denial easier and sea control harder. Perhaps all surface vessels—for war as well as for trade—will become (are becoming?) vulnerable. This consideration also points toward the possibility of, and need for, cooperative maritime security, even between the established and rising sea power, which the next chapter will explore.

CHAPTER FIVE
Regional Maritime Security

"Aim to be statesmen as well as seamen."—A. T. Mahan[1]

Mahan Versus Mullen

If concentrated surface power was Mahan's prescription, competitive great-power politics was his premise. The preceding chapter indicates that concentrated surface power has been overtaken by the information revolution. This chapter explores whether the premise of great-power competition necessarily remains valid.

Recall that Mahan was a son of the century of Darwin and Bismarck, of ambitious nation-states pitted against one another, strength on strength. The race for possessions and resources—imperialism—globalized their competition. Industrialization both expanded sea-borne trade and furnished the resources to build strong modern navies to protect or disrupt that trade. Common interests in trade were subordinate to mercantilist impulses, whereby one state's success was thought to come at the expense of the success of others. In such a climate, the only assurance of maritime security was independent national sea power (sea control), which could also be used to degrade the maritime security of others (sea denial). Because the fittest power, Britain, could dominate weaker ones—Holland, Spain, Russia, and France—superiority at sea meant dominance at sea. Therefore, emerging powers that depended on trade and aspired to be imperial powers—America, Germany, and Japan—had not only to become sea powers but also to challenge if not confront the established sea power.

[1] Alfred T. Mahan, *Naval Strategy*, quoted in Hattendorf, 1991, p. 21.

Mahan's ideas were informed by what he observed of British sea power and, in turn, applied by Americans, Germans, and Japanese to motivate and guide dramatic naval expansion.

A century-plus later, another American naval officer, Admiral Mike Mullen, while serving as Chief of Naval Operations, offered a fundamentally different idea in the fundamentally different world he observed. The integration of the world economy in the late 20th century caused another burst of international trade, 90 percent of which is by sea. As global markets and global industries formed, economic interdependence has deepened. In these conditions, the health of national economies depends more than ever on the health of the world economy in which they are a part. So the success of one power correlates with the success of other powers, not their failure. More and more nations are joining the mainstream of economic development, trade, and interdependence. There is a greater awareness of common interests in the efficient and safe trade of materials, food, fuels, and goods.

While contemporary sea powers—the United States, above all—have the means to disrupt the trade of others, economic integration has made it self-defeating to do so. More plausible threats now come from those few states and many non-state actors who would threaten or abuse the expansion of trade: pirates, terrorists, and traffickers in drugs, weapons of mass destruction, and human beings. In addition, resources located in and under the oceans are in growing demand to maintain economic health in the advanced North and nourish rapid growth in the developing South. Finally, with coastal populations expanding rapidly and under growing danger of disasters and rising sea levels, natural maritime threats have grown along with human threats. For these reasons, there is growing support for the idea that the seas are "commons" in need of joint stewardship and security by the states and enterprises that use them for good purposes.

The main steward of the commons, naturally, would be the United States, sole superpower and dominant sea power. But unlike Britain's unilateral command of the seas in the 19th century, the United States will lead a multilateral approach. With the Cold War behind it, the United States has steadily reduced its fleet. As more of the world's seas need more security, as a result of globalization and expanded trade, the United States cannot afford to perform in the 21st century the role Great Britain played in the 19th. Whereas sea power is an important aspect of American power now, it was the foundation of British power then. (Even at that, recall that, by the beginning of the 20th century, domestic economic demands were threatening the affordability of Britain continuing to "rule the waves.") The number of ships in the U.S. Navy of 2000 was one-third that of the Royal Navy of 1900. With climbing capital costs and operating expenses (e.g., fuel), odds are against the U.S. Navy expanding.

In these circumstances, Mullen's idea was a simple one: All like-minded nations with a requirement for maritime security should become members of a global coalition.[2] The United States should organize and lead a "Thousand-Ship Navy"—officially, the "Global Maritime Partnership Initiative"—consisting of warships, coast guards, tankers, freighters, and all other flagged vessels that could assist in monitoring and policing the world's waters. Advanced information technology would network participating fleets and vessels in what some have referred to as a "global" or "post-modern" navy.[3]

In Mullen's words:

> Imagine [a] fleet operating with the navies . . . of a host of other nations, fully netted and interoperable. They could be anywhere the national and international political leadership wanted them to be . . . ready to go at a moment's notice. Not just a force to wage war, but a force to wage peace as well.[4]

While the rhetoric of the Thousand-Ship Navy has cooled off and the terminology has changed—new leaders like new slogans—the basic

---

[2] The Mullen initiative was criticized in conservative and traditional naval circles as naïve at best and a smokescreen to cover the poor stewardship that allowed the U.S. Navy to shrink.

[3] Richard A. Bitzinger, "Recent Developments in Naval and Maritime Modernization in the Asia-Pacific: Implications for Regional Security," in Saunders et al., eds., 2011, p. 38.

[4] Mullen, 2005.

idea continues to affect not only the U.S. Navy but many others, including in the Western Pacific.[5]

Regional partnerships are forming in Africa, Latin America, and Southeast Asia, mostly at U.S. encouragement. Their purposes range from protection of littoral waters (off West Africa) to counter-drug patrolling (in the Caribbean) to WMD interdiction and choke-point security (the Strait of Malacca). Even as the U.S. Navy maintains its blue-water supremacy, despite declining fleet size, it is developing its green-water capabilities with the Littoral Combat Ship and new high-speed vessels to facilitate working with partners. Although the U.S. Global Maritime Partnership Initiative was motivated by the general problem of maritime security, the cause of cooperation got a big boost with the spread of terrorism, the rise of piracy, and several huge coastal natural disasters in the first decade of the 21st century.

Even the recruiting slogan of today's U.S. Navy—"A Global Force for Good"—implies a preference for engagement and cooperation over naval warfare (albeit with a reminder of U.S. power and reach). Cynics might say that the U.S. Navy fashioned the idea of American-led cooperative maritime security to justify maintaining and modernizing the fleet as it became clear that it has no serious opponent. But the underlying premise—too much ocean, too many choke-points, too many threats, too few navy ships—is incontestable when considering the vital importance of oceanic trade to the world and U.S. economies.

Lately, the prospect of warfare from and on the sea has returned, especially in Middle East and East Asian waters of strategic importance. U.S. defense strategy concentrates increasingly on major military contingencies that could place heavy demands on naval forces for traditional missions: sea control, sea denial, and strike. In particular, the growing anti-naval and naval capabilities of China in the Western Pacific and Iran in the Persian Gulf command the top attention of the U.S. government, not just the Navy. Because the United States does not anticipate large-scale land-warfare with Iran, much less with China, maritime war-fighting capabilities, such as for sea-based strike,

---

5 See, for example, Chris Rahman, *The Global Maritime Partnership Initiative: Implications for the Royal Australian Navy*, Australian Department of Defence, 2008.

are considered key. Hence, Mullen's maritime partnership now competes with Mahan-like (or Mahan-lite?) sea power as the basis for naval planning, fleet architecture, and politics.

While the U.S. Navy is extraordinarily versatile and resourceful, there is no denying that the forces and competencies best suited for maritime cooperation (green-water engagement) are not the same as those most needed for maritime warfare against capable states (blue-water control, denial, and strike). U.S. sea power is thus being pulled in two directions: collaborative and competitive. This naval tug-of-war is putting operational strains on existing forces, intensifying competition over investment, and creating tension between openly sharing information with many partners and restricting information to only the closest allies. Aggravating the U.S. Navy's resource dilemma is the fact that it, along with the U.S. Air Force, has been the post-9/11 "bill-payer" of U.S. requirements to expand and operate the Army and Marine Corps for occupation and counterinsurgency in Iraq and Afghanistan. U.S. defense spending has grown enormously since 2001, but funding for naval modernization has been more or less flat. So the need to partner with other navies remains strong.

While the Navy tries to reconcile the two, it is best to acknowledge that Mullen's imperative of cooperation largely contradicts Mahan's inevitability of competition—which helps explain why a fleet optimized for the latter is not optimal for the former.[6] Therefore, the validity of the underlying theories needs to be examined. Has mutual responsibility for the commons replaced the drive for advantage? Is there more to the idea of partnership than a situational need to make up for the post–Cold War contraction of the U.S. Navy in the absence of a rival sea power? And, for this study, is there some way the United States and China can snatch the promise of maritime partnership from the jaws of sea-power confrontation?

---

[6] To be fair to Mullen and other uniformed advocates of cooperative maritime security, they have not argued that the United States could or should relinquish its position as the world's dominant sea power in order to pursue multilateral solutions, or that multilateral solutions were necessitated by U.S. inability to remain the dominant sea power. Rather, the idea is that being the dominant sea power allows the United States to lead multilateral solutions.

If we are indeed in for a change in the basic premise of sea power, the main reason would be that globalization is making cooperative maritime security more attractive and even compelling. But why would globalization favor cooperation over confrontation at sea? This is a legitimate question: After all, economic interdependence did not prevent naval rivalry or, for that matter, world war a century ago. More to the point at hand, why would the common economic interests of China and the United States, including secure trade, foster maritime cooperation when such an approach was not pursued by Great Britain and Germany, also major trading partners when they became rival sea powers? The answer is complex but worth examining.

First, it can be argued that although economic interdependence did not prevent the great-power politics and antagonism that led to World War I, *it should have.* World War I was a tragic triumph of jealousy, hubris, and maneuvering over the modernizing and presumed moderating effects of increasingly interconnected economies. Sovereigns made win-or-lose calculations that had lose-lose consequences for their societies. While some powers paid a higher price than others for World War I, losses suffered by "winners" were also staggering (enough to nurture British and French appeasement of Hitler). Moreover, the automaticity built into pre-war alliances and interlocking pledges of support in the event of war—later seen as regrettable—left decision-makers with little space or time to manage a cascade of crises that led to war despite their inhibitions. Had European statesmen understood how long and devastating the War would be, even for winners, they just might have exercised better control over their mechanistic alignments, military planning triggers, and optimistic generals. That German leaders, for example, did not foresee how war would turn beneficial economic cooperation into ruinous economic punishment is not a reason to expect leaders today to be as myopic. Likewise, that British leaders saw no alternative but to deny Germany's maritime-security interests does not mean that no alternative to sea-power rivalry exists today—or, for that matter, existed then.

In this regard, and second, it is evident that today's Chinese and American leaders *do* appreciate that conflict could inflict great economic harm, all the more so because of Sino-U.S. interdependence.

When crises have occurred (e.g., over Taiwan or U.S. surveillance patrols near China), one or both capitals have acted judiciously. Such care by each power toward the other, despite divergent interests in the region, is not only because of doubts about the course and outcome of military conflict but also because both economies could suffer tremendously regardless. Thus, the fact that the Chinese and American economies are coupled and largely share the same fate, in war as in peace, *is* a major inhibition on great-power behavior.[7] Conversely, if Sino-U.S. war were to occur, it could be because of the same sort of miscalculation or conceit that befell European leaders a century ago.

Third, the nature and workings of economic integration under conditions of Europe prior to World War I are different *in kind* than those of globalization.[8] The former involved choices at the margin to acquire raw materials and goods from nations where a comparative advantage in producing them existed. Although there was significant international investment, trade was largely replaceable and reversible, albeit at considerable cost. Under today's conditions of an integrated world economy, interdependence is becoming organic: Markets for goods, services, capital, finance, technology, management, distribution, production operations, infrastructure, and equity are increasingly global and unified. Movements through these markets are continuous, swift, and resistant to national control. Market-driven value chains—research, development, componentry, sub-systems, systems, services—do not respect sovereign jurisdictions or preferences. This is structurally different than interacting national economies. If the breakdown of *international* trade and investment due to war and protectionism harmed all national economies during World War I and the Depression, the damage from the collapse of today's *global* economy would be incalculable.

---

7 Arguably, the prospect of "mutual assured economic destruction" (a term coined by Jim Dobbins) is playing in the Sino-American case the role mutual assured nuclear destruction played in the Soviet-American case. (See Dobbins et al., 2011.)

8 See Raymond Vernon's *Sovereignty at Bay: The Multinational Spread of U.S. Enterprises* for a powerful analysis of why and how economic interdependence under conditions of "globalization" is more constraining on nations than the interdependence among European nations prior to World War I.

Globalization does not merely connect such economies as those of the United States and China, it mixes and melds them. It not only leaves sovereigns with diminished control but also vests in them a shared vital interest in sustaining and protecting their common economy. One aspect of this interest is the security of the seas on which the bulk of the commerce of the increasingly common world economy takes place. This does not guarantee that powers will not compete at sea. Indeed, growing maritime rivalry and tension in East Asia is proof that they *will.* Although certain aspects of Mahan's teachings now seem quaint, his premise that relative sea power matters still stands. Yet, globalization means that cooperative maritime security stands a better chance of overcoming rivalry today than it did, say, in the Anglo-German case of 1890–1914.

Maritime Security and East Asia

What does this trade-off between competitive and cooperative sea power imply for the Western Pacific today and in the future? In a nutshell, Sino-U.S. maritime cooperation could, *under certain conditions*, serve U.S. security interests, sustain U.S. influence, bolster confidence and stability, reduce risks of conflict, and foster wider Sino-U.S. cooperation in this critical and uncertain region. Moreover, it could serve Chinese interests better than competition or confrontation at sea with the United States (though, as we will see, the Chinese might disagree).

To review: The United States can and should capitalize on its current military-technological advantages; however, it cannot count on those advantages to maintain sea control and thus protect its interests in the Western Pacific. Air-Sea Battle could be destabilizing and will not preserve the survivability of U.S. surface naval-strike forces, e.g., carriers, unless China's anti-naval kill-chain is preemptively attacked and largely destroyed. The United States can and should begin to shift from reliance on a traditional surface fleet to a more distributed, elusive, diverse, and survivable version of sea power. Yet, such revolutionary change, though technologically feasible, is unrealistic politically and institutionally. Moreover, while it could take China decades to build a first-tier blue-water navy, it can achieve a measure of sea denial with anti-naval capabilities much sooner. In the face of this challenge to U.S. sea power in the Western Pacific, the option of strengthening deterrence by relying increasingly on the threat of escalation involves growing risks for the United States. Thus, the United States is in a strategic predicament: It cannot let China create a prejudicial sphere of influence in this important region; yet, the sea power on which its access, influence, and security depend will become increasingly vulnerable and tenuous.

More generally, technological trends are making sea control (assuring access) harder and sea denial (interrupting access) easier. Capabilities to target and strike surface vessels from above (missiles) or below (submarines) will steadily undermine maritime security for both the United States and China, along with other nations that depend on sea-borne trade and free navigation. The growing vulnerability of surface fleets and shipping in general could undercut Mahan's premise that powerful states that depend on trade are preordained to compete. In time, all states, including the United States and China, should have an interest in preventing attacks on increasingly vulnerable surface vessels. For now, the Chinese are placing their bets on anti-naval and other A2AD capabilities to neutralize the U.S. strike threat they perceive. Yet, the targeting technologies that "go around, come around." By the time China can build and operate a genuine blue-water navy, the result will be at risk. Given the costs and the prospective vulnerability of surface fleets, China's civilian leaders, if not necessarily its military leaders, should be at least as concerned as their American counterparts about the prospect of sea denial. At some point, because of growing vulnerabilities, common interest in maritime security could outweigh competitive instincts.

A contest between Mahan's theory of competition and Mullen's appeal for cooperation is already evident in East Asia. With the growth of Chinese anti-naval and naval capabilities, as already detailed, U.S. sea power is being contested. At the same time, non-state threats, illicit trafficking, resource disputes, and risky incidents-at-sea call for cooperative security among all states with a stake and capabilities in the Western Pacific. In fact, the idea of cooperative maritime security in the

Western Pacific is starting to gather interest, especially among China's Southeast Asian neighbors and the United States.[9] If and as such cooperation develops in the region, the key question will be whether it includes or is instead aligned against China. The United States should leave that choice to China, though it should try to encourage the Chinese to participate.

The possibility of Sino-American maritime partnership depends heavily on other states of the region, for they will have a voice and role. As China has expanded and extended its military capabilities, its Asian neighbors have responded by improving theirs.[10] While navies elsewhere are barely being maintained, East Asian nations, especially allies and partners of the United States, are building some of the world's most advanced:[11]

- Australia has undergone a transformation in defense concepts and capabilities, from static continental defense to power-projection missions stressing expeditionary forces, mobility, precision strike, jointness, and networking. The Royal Australian Navy's modernization is now a national priority, with more and better surface combatants, submarines, missile-defense ships, amphibious-assault ships, and, tying them together, advanced C4ISR. The Australian and U.S. navies are working closely together operationally and in sharing sophisticated technology.
- Japan is in a period of naval expansion, coinciding with a general toughening of security policy owing to concerns about Chinese power in the region and American commitment to the region. The Japanese Maritime Self-Defense Force "has greatly increased its expeditionary capabilities, firepower, and C4ISR [and] is now larger than the British Royal Navy."[12] In addition to acquiring

9 Singapore, Malaysia, and Indonesia are pursuing partnering.

10 East Asian concerns about growing Chinese power and assertiveness have been compounded by creeping doubts about American steadfastness, especially during its post-9/11 decade-long preoccupation with violent Islamism in other regions.

11 See Bitzinger, 2011.

12 Bitzinger, 2011.

new surface combatants, it is emphasizing advanced submarines, high-speed logistics ships, missile-defense ships, and amphibious ships. Though still mainly defensive in mission, Japanese naval forces will increasingly provide a critical "shield" while the U.S. Navy provides the "spear" in combined operations. Reacting to China's expanding sea-power strategy, the latest Japanese Defense White Paper warns that Japan will not be passive.[13] (The Japanese also express doubts about whether the PLA and PLAN are under firm political control.)

- While maintaining ground and air forces capable of defeating North Korea's decaying conventional forces, South Korea has begun to expand and improve its naval forces for missions beyond the Peninsula. The Republic of Korea Navy is graduating from coastal defense to an all-purpose oceangoing fleet, with advanced submarines, surface combatants (with anti-ship and land-attack cruise missiles), and amphibious ships. While seeking to reduce its naval dependence on the United States, South Korea has in fact moved even closer as a result of North Korean maritime provocations.
- Singapore, Malaysia, Indonesia, and Vietnam are all improving their navies, though at different rates and with different priorities. Singapore's navy, though small, is becoming one of the world's most advanced and benefits from a comparatively large ($9 billion) defense budget. The requirement to protect sea approaches and regional check-points is being met by increasingly advanced and networked platforms. Indonesia is improving its green-water capabilities (for reasons the map would suggest). As the PLAN becomes more threatening in the South China Sea, naval cooperation between these states and the United States has grown.
- India is in the midst of modernizing its large navy. It has a full assortment of surface combatants, including aircraft carriers, and is expanding and upgrading its submarine force. Though becoming more powerful, the Indian navy is concerned mainly with a

[13] "Tokyo Seeks to Expand Defense Against China," *Wall Street Journal*, July 12, 2012, p. 14.

"constabulary role" in the Indian Ocean (on which 90 percent of its trade moves). At the same time, China and India clearly keep an eye on one another's growing sea power as each develops its own.

The United States has good relations with all these countries. Even with those that are not formal allies or historical friends—India and Vietnam, for instance—U.S. security cooperation is expanding, mainly because of overlapping concerns about China. Bilateral cooperation encompasses and in some cases prominently features naval collaboration, ranging from the sharing of sensitive technology and operational information (in the cases of Japan, South Korea, and Australia) to support for improvement of indigenous capabilities. Among the ways the United States could bolster the contribution of the security partners to deterrence and defense in the region is to enhance their anti-naval capabilities, e.g., land- or ship-based missiles, in order to raise the costs of Chinese force projection in the same way China is raising the costs of U.S. force projection in the region.

Although naval/anti-naval technology trends are unfavorable to U.S. sea power in East Asia, the improved capabilities of key states that look to the United States for leadership can be a major geo-strategic asset vis-à-vis China's growing power. This assumes, of course, that the United States retains their trust by maintaining its power and backing its friends in the region when China attempts to coerce them. It also assumes that the American statesmen and military leaders will be skillful enough to strengthen and expand U.S. security relationships in a way that incentivizes Chinese moderation rather than Chinese hostility. At the same time, the United States cannot fail to support and receive support from its allies and partners out of fear that China will disapprove.

Although there is a regional preference for U.S. power and tentative multilateral cooperation, the United States has no Western Pacific alliance like NATO—and no prospect for one—on which to organize a maritime alliance. China exhibits neither the revolutionary zealotry nor the expansionist drive that the Soviet Union had (in its prime) and that made NATO a requirement in Europe. Moreover, while the Soviet

Union was economically and politically completely isolated from Western Europe, China is an inseparable part of East Asia—economically, culturally, and demographically. Barring a burst of Chinese aggressiveness, a U.S.-led NATO-like structure for East Asia is neither advisable nor feasible. Nevertheless, with growing regional naval capabilities and concern about China, it might be possible for the United States to institutionalize multilateral maritime security—an East Asian maritime partnership—involving the countries mentioned above and most others.

Generally, the United States has found that its Global Maritime Partnership Initiative has branched into regional endeavors. This comes as no surprise, given that most nations' maritime interests are more local or regional than global. Because, again, East Asia is a virtual archipelago—with some of the world's most important and interdependent economies spanning some of the world's most important seas—it could be argued that no region has a greater need for a multilateral approach to maritime security. Moreover, because the region's main seafaring nations are prosperous and have competent navies, it is only reasonable that they should do their fair share in collectively securing waters that are at least as important to them as to the United States.

Of course, the idea of creating an East Asia maritime security partnership raises the question of its relation to China. The argument for excluding China is that its own naval and anti-naval capabilities and activities are the principal threats that would prompt its neighbors to join the United States in multilateral maritime security. By this reasoning, such a maritime security grouping would be a naval *alliance* against China. However, aligning the region against China could result in economic protectionism, accelerated Chinese anti-access efforts, increased risk of conflict, and diminished maritime security. Moreover, while China's neighbors are anxious about China's capabilities and conduct, especially at sea, it is doubtful that they would want to organize against it, with or without the United States.

The argument for including China is twofold. First, it would allay Chinese suspicion that the true goals of the United States in the region are China's encirclement and containment. Second, with China being such an important trading partner of all the prospective participants in such a regional grouping, its exclusion from an attempt to secure regional trade would be anomalous and unproductive. Unlike the Soviet Union's isolation to Europe, China is an integral part of the region and its economy. Security of regional sea-borne trade and security of sea-borne trade with China are completely entangled.

Under the right conditions, including China in a multilateral East Asian maritime partnership could have a salutary effect on security at sea, on regional security in general, and on U.S. interests. Better to bring inside than leave outside the rising power with capacities to either improve or degrade maritime security. More generally, better to increase China's stake in regional arrangements than to cement its isolation and cause it to become revisionist.

Assuming that China would be invited to join it, the question then arises as to what threat, if not China, would motivate the formation of the grouping. As already noted, the Mullen idea addressed both non-state threats to maritime security and dangerous or harmful sea trafficking by states and non-states. Apart from such external threats, an East Asian maritime partnership including China would constitute a sort of collective security arrangement—one with a circumscribed purpose and scope: to provide maritime security. Generally speaking, collective security is different in kind than a security alliance in that it includes all states in a given geographic domain, whether friendly or not. It is undergirded by an understanding that all participating states will refrain from force and other aggressive conduct. Further, it is disciplined by a corresponding understanding—at least an implication—that the participants will organize and may act against any state that violates the collective security, even if that state had acceded to the grouping. In effect, a collective security arrangement can be transformed into an alliance against any wayward participant.[14]

---

[14] The idea of collective security is an old one. Cardinal Richelieu proposed one for Europe in 1629, elements of which were included in the Treaty of Westphalia, in which all European nation-states joined in pledging to respect each other's sovereignty and security. The League of Nations and the United Nations had elements of collective security, though the former had no teeth and the latter permits a veto.

In the case of East Asia, a *comprehensive* collective security arrangement would be practically impossible to form under current conditions. For one thing, China would oppose absolutely any implication that the Taiwan problem is a matter of international security and any attempt to limit its options, including the use of force. Yet this does not preclude an agreement focused on the avoidance of force in international waters and, importantly, in disputed waters. While states with claims would resist any arrangement that would weaken those claims, they would be expected to affirm the widely accepted norm that disputes should not be settled by force.

Along this line, the United States could propose—others in the region would of course need to agree—that China be invited and urged to join a maritime security partnership provided certain criteria are met, not only by China but by all participants. The matter of criteria thus becomes dispositive.[15] While the United States and its partners would want to facilitate China's involvement, they would also want to ensure that the goals of regional maritime security are served. To this end, all states wishing to join an East Asian maritime partnership, including the two great powers, might be expected to agree

- to settle maritime territorial and resource disputes peacefully, consensually, and through international legal norms and means
- not to use force against commercial and other civilian shipping engaged in peacetime trade and other peaceful activities
- that the United States and other countries not located in the region have as much right of access to East Asian waters as any country of the region
- to institute information-sharing, crisis consultations, confidence-building measures, joint exercises, and joint operations
- to take appropriate joint action against non-state actors or states that violate these norms.

---

[15] In the trade field, the U.S.-backed Trans-Pacific Partnership has made Chinese participation possible but set such a high bar for eligibility that the Chinese regard it as a U.S. scheme to exclude China from arrangements that will increase U.S. benefits from East Asia's economic dynamism. This is *not* the way the United States would want the Chinese to interpret a regional maritime security proposal.

Such undertakings are consistent with established international norms, including peaceful dispute settlement, protection from attack of non-combatants, and freedom of navigation in international waters. Nevertheless, there is benefit in reiterating them in this particular regional setting. Moreover, it could be beneficial to reinforce these norms with practical cooperative measures and with agreement to cooperate against those that flout them.

The Chinese would be especially wary of any provision prejudicial to their claims—indeed, their insistence—that certain islands (in some cases, little more than rocks) in the South China and East China Seas are theirs, based on historical possession. The positions of China, Taiwan, Vietnam, the Philippines, Brunei, and Indonesia regarding the South China Sea are exceedingly complex and seemingly irreconcilable; and those of China, Taiwan, and Japan in the East China Sea are nearly so. Resolution of these disputes should not be a precondition of forming or joining an East Asian maritime partnership. Indeed, so complicated and unclear are the merits of the welter of claims, especially in the South China Sea, that making their resolution a precondition of regional maritime partnership would mount to deferring this idea indefinitely. If any state—whether a U.S. ally or China—sought American endorsement of its legal position in return for its support for an East Asian maritime partnership, the United States should decline (as it now declines to take sides). It would be essential to show China both that such a partnership will not be used against it and that it cannot be used by them against other claimants.

Even such circumscribed purposes could be difficult to fulfill, because one party's failure to contest another's military or economic activities may be prejudicial to its legal case. Nonetheless, precisely because the scramble for islands, waters, and resources in East Asian waters is already harmful to both economic development and security, a general pledge to act peacefully and cooperatively ought to be a criterion of a regional collective maritime security regime.[16]

---

[16] The idea of a code of conduct for the South China Sea has garnered interest from time to time. This is not to be confused with a definitive settlement of the disputes themselves. One of the main impediments to progress even toward a general code of conduct is Chinese insis-

The Chinese could be attracted to an assurance that participating states would not attack its commercial shipping, since this would give it some confidence that its access to the oceans of the region and the world would not be cut off, especially by the United States. Of course, they would be unlikely to rely absolutely on such an assurance and so would presumably continue to expand China's naval power. For its part, the United States would have to consider whether a pledge not to attack commercial shipping would forfeit an important option. However, as the study of international law and the history of warfare show, what nations do when at war is constrained by a different set of norms than the standards they observe in peacetime. The United States does not currently claim the right to attack commercial shipping engaged in peacetime, peaceful activity.

A sincere invitation to join on such terms would leave China with the choice of whether to enhance maritime security cooperatively or else risk the partnership becoming an anti-China naval alliance. There are at least three possible results: China could decline and reject the grouping as anti-Chinese; it could join but then fail to adhere to the criteria; or it could accept the criteria, join, and become a valued partner. The United States should aim for the third possibility. Of course, gaining Chinese acceptance would be a tall order. Knowing as they do regional and U.S. attitudes about the growth of China's power, the Chinese will be instinctively suspicious that the strategic motivation behind the initiative is to constrain China's use of that power. Moreover, in surveying the prospective membership, the Chinese will surely notice that the most important members are either U.S. allies or drawing closer to the United States, which would imply that China could be as regularly opposed inside the collectivity as it would by remaining outside. Finally, even if Chinese political and business leaders saw advantages in joining, the PLA would see more cons than pros, and it is not clear that the civilian government is prepared to overrule the military. The history of Sino-U.S. military-to-military engagement is not

---

tence that arrangements be worked out *bilaterally*, which would of course work to China's advantage and exclude the United States and other external actors and organizations.

encouraging, but neither does it suggest that the pursuit of maritime cooperation is bound to be fruitless.

Sino-American Security Cooperation: Rocky Path or Barren Soil

Four decades of U.S. efforts to engage China in military and security cooperation can best be described as disappointing, except when the Chinese saw important concrete gains to be had. Sino-U.S. rapprochement, starting with Nixon's visit to China, led to significant military contacts, arms sales, intelligence sharing, and other forms of cooperation. When the object of that cooperation, the Soviet bloc, collapsed in 1989, the enthusiasm on both sides was dampened. That same year, the attack by Chinese security forces on peaceful pro-democracy demonstrators in Tiananmen Square caused the United States to break off such activities.

Since then, the United States has tried repeatedly and earnestly to create channels of communication on security matters in hopes of reducing mistrust, avoiding miscalculation, and preventing mistakes (e.g., incidents at sea). While naval topics and navy-to-navy contacts are only a part of the wider U.S. approach, they are obviously important because of the growing overlap of Chinese and American sea power in the same East Asian waters. The main modalities have been visits and meetings of leaders, defense officials, and officers. But the United States has also promoted warship port-calls and operational cooperation. The only notable instance of maritime cooperation has occurred far from the region, countering Somali pirates.

Generally speaking, the Chinese attitude toward security cooperation has been hesitant, ambivalent, and conditional. After agreeing to contacts, the Chinese then suspend them when faced with what they deem American effrontery, e.g., by U.S. arms sales to Taiwan and support for Chinese dissidents or alleged separatists (e.g., the Dalai Lama). American officials and observers now wonder whether the main effect of U.S. efforts to engage Chinese counterparts has been to hand the

Chinese leverage on other issues in the relationship.[17] On the whole, senior U.S. officers have reason to feel that they have gone the extra mile to engage China, only to be frustrated.

The PLA Navy has been among the organizations least interested and involved in the on-again/off-again contacts that do occur. Reminiscent of German and Japanese admirals of old, Chinese naval leaders have been especially outspoken about China's maritime ambitions and prerogatives. When China has made provocative moves in the East China Sea and South China Sea, or has reacted strongly to what it perceives as provocations by others, the PLAN is the agent, if not the mastermind. Thus, the Chinese military service that is most likely to cause a confrontation with American sea power in the Western Pacific, and arguably the most important to engage, has been the least forthcoming and most obstreperous. Because the Chinese Navy's plans and programs depend on regarding the U.S. Navy as an enemy of and threat to China, its interest is not in engaging in maritime cooperation but rather in foiling it. Like the German admirals in the late 19th century, Chinese admirals rest their case on the intention of the established sea power to deny their country its rightful access. This suggests that maritime security could be among the least conducive areas for cooperation.

What, then, would make one think that collaboration in maritime security has *any* chance of success? Clearly, it will not happen without innovative U.S. leadership. In particular, the United States should shape conditions by pursuing an East Asian maritime partnership with or without China. This would provide the United States with leverage it now lacks. The goal, once again, is Chinese involvement, which would address maritime security and help sustain U.S. sea power in the Western Pacific. If the Chinese elected to remain apart, despite a sincere offer to participate, this would give the United States and its other partners all the more reason to view China as a potentially unhelpful or threatening actor in regional maritime security.

Herein lies the main reason why the Chinese could be hesitant to reject categorically participating in a maritime collective-security regime: fear of regional isolation. Even as China's military capabili-

---

17 O'Rourke, 2011.

ties have grown—and before the United States signaled in 2012 the renewal of its commitment to East Asia—key states of the region have become wary of the former and edged closer to the latter. This has led to the paradoxical possibility of China becoming both more powerful and more isolated. It is hard to believe that China's political leaders and economic elites regard this as optimal.

The mixed reaction of the Chinese to the 2012 U.S. strategic pivot to East Asia could be indicative of how they see the tension between their objectives and pitfalls in the region. American China-watchers have diagnosed that reaction this way:[18]

- Official Chinese comments were low-key, low-level, and muted. Quasi-official, military, media, and think-tank opinions were generally more critical and more pointed.
- Foreign Ministry spokespersons stressed U.S. assurances of friendly intentions and acceptance of China's rise, as well as China's hope that closer cooperation would result from a reinvigoration of U.S. interests in the region.
- Three factors that help explain the ambivalent and cautious Chinese official reaction are (a) an aversion to roiling relations with the United States on the eve of China's leadership succession; (b) a belief that long-term trends are in China's favor, so it should remain calm; and (c) fear of isolation in the region.

This last observation is especially noteworthy here. The Chinese—at least *some* Chinese—believe that the country's increased forcefulness in recent years has caused the region's other important states to seek the shelter of U.S. security links. U.S. relations have strengthened with South Korea, Japan, Vietnam, Indonesia, Australia, New Zealand, and others—even Burma. Meanwhile, North Korea has become less an ally than a liability—a growing one, at that. Astute Chinese analysts, and probably the Foreign Ministry, realize that the U.S. pivot is largely

---

[18] See Michael D. Swaine, "Chinese Leadership and Elite Responses to the U.S. Pacific Pivot," *China Leadership Monitor*, No. 38, Summer 2012; Bonnie Glazer and Brittany Billingsley, "U.S. Pivot to Asia Leaves China Off Balance," *Comparative Connections: A Tri-annual E-Journal on East Asian Bilateral Relations*, January 2012.

a response to regional anxiety brought on by China itself, and thus embraced by virtually the entire region. For China to react with hostility to the pivot and toward the United States would validate and reinforce the regional concerns that led to the pivot in the first place. As one U.S. expert observes: "A number of Chinese analysts argue that China should bear some responsibility for the resurgence of U.S. influence and power around its periphery."[19]

This insight into the worries of the Chinese is confirmed by how emphatically they warn against U.S. attempts at dividing the region, which is Chinese code for isolating China. In fact, China's own conduct has had more to do with its isolation than American conduct has, given the U.S. post-9/11 preoccupations in the Middle East and South Asia. It follows that China's opposition to U.S. policies that respond to regional security concerns could increase, not reduce, its isolation. This consideration is unlikely to weigh enough to offset Chinese hostility toward U.S. moves, especially military enhancements, potentially threatening to China. Seen in this light, *if* all important states in the region welcomed a U.S. multilateral maritime-security plan, *if* such an initiative was not militarily threatening, *if* the United States expressed a sincere and strong interest in China's involvement, and *if* the Chinese knew they had no veto, then they might be hesitant to reject it lest doing so add to their isolation.

As David Shlapak of RAND has reminded the author, the Chinese *already* expect most important East Asian states to seek close ties with the United States, if they do not already have them. Regional concerns about China are an inevitable result of China's growing power—a price that must be paid in order to protect and advance China's legitimate interests now that China, at long last, has the means. By this reasoning, the Chinese already discount the possibility of further isolation, thus mooting the political disadvantage of refusing to participate in collective maritime security. Maybe so; however, there are hints that not all Chinese see it this way, as noted above. Moreover, why give the Americans and their allies another opportunity to align the region against China when an opportunity to reduce China's isolation pres-

[19] Glazer and Billingsley, 2012, p. 4.

ents itself? Of course, this assumes that the Chinese see an invitation to participate as honest and non-prejudicial.

Even if the Chinese see risks in refusing regional maritime security cooperation, they would suspect a Trojan Horse (or Sea Horse?) aimed at shoring up the political foundation for U.S. military presence and alliances surrounding China. While professing to want good relations with the United States and to accept the United States as a Pacific power, they feel threatened both by U.S. military capabilities and by U.S. alliances, old and new.[20] But as long as the U.S. initiative was cast as a way of involving China in regional security, not embarrassing China, those Chinese most concerned about isolation (e.g., diplomats) might prevail over those who reflexively oppose U.S. forces, relationships, and policies in the region (e.g., PLA brass).

More likely, the Chinese would be divided over the propositions advanced here. In a classic damned-if-you-do/damned-if-you-don't bind, they would not want to give legitimacy to U.S. leadership and sea power in East Asia, yet they would not want to give the Americans an opening to organize most of East Asia against them at sea. The Chinese might lobby their neighbors to rebuff the American plan; but in view of regional attitudes about Chinese maritime ambitions, they would not likely succeed.

The approach would only work if U.S. civilian leaders appealed to their Chinese counterparts—both political and economic elites—in the interest of common maritime security. U.S. naval and other military leaders should of course present the idea in the most forthcoming way they can to their Chinese counterparts. But American diplomacy on this should avoid handing the PLA a veto (if it does not already have one on such a matter). British statesmen did not reach out wholeheartedly to their German counterparts to head off a naval rivalry, leaving it to intermediaries to test the waters, so to speak.

In that case, not only did the British admiralty enjoy great political influence, but the commitment to sea-power dominance was engrained

---

[20] For the latest and an excellent version of the view that China is essentially defensive and feels threatened, see Andrew Nathan and Andrew Scobell, "How China Sees America," *Foreign Affairs,* September/October 2012.

in national consciousness and policy. British politicians and industrialists saw the world and the need to block Germany more or less the same as the Royal Navy did. Their German counterparts, especially Kaiser Wilhelm, were no less deferential to their own admirals. Comparatively, U.S. political leaders are not beholden to "naval interests." Moreover, U.S. naval leaders such as Mullen are on record favoring collective maritime security, including with China. Because regional maritime cooperation, with or without China, would not diminish or replace U.S. sea power in the Western Pacific but rather help to sustain it, the U.S. Navy should support this initiative. Whether China's leaders are as taken with the logic of adversarial sea power as Imperial Germany's were is less clear—but worth testing.

The United States has recently raised its sights and sought to broaden the scope for Sino-American security dialogue to encompass increasingly difficult regional, nuclear, space, cyber, and maritime matters. In this context, the United States could introduce at the highest political levels the idea of Sino-American maritime partnership. This alone will not bring the Chinese along. What could do so is confronting Chinese leaders with the prospects of self-exclusion from regional partnership. Whether they could bring along the PLA and PLAN is unclear.

In this regard, one possible straw in the wind is a reported recent agreement between PACOM and the PLAN to discuss logistics cooperation in cases of cooperative missions to combat piracy and provide humanitarian relief in the event of natural disasters.[21] Obviously, the Chinese have more to gain than their American counterparts in practical terms. Moreover, this is a far cry from general agreement on cooperative maritime security. Still, it suggests that navy-to-navy collaboration is not taboo for the Chinese.

In no case can the United States mortgage its ability to defend its interests, its allies, its forces, freedom of the seas, and commercial shipping throughout the region. Cooperation with the region's capable seafaring states would be advantageous for the United States in any case—

---

21 See Donna Miles, "U.S., China to Consider Sharing Resources During Joint Missions," Armed Forces Press Service, October 12, 2012.

whether one adheres to the view of Mahan, Mullen, or both. Indeed, East Asian maritime partnership would become the new framework in which U.S. sea power would remain in the region. Moreover, whether China participated or not, the United States should retain and modernize its naval capabilities for war-fighting, along the lines recommended in the preceding chapter.

Of course, China would be no more likely than the United States to treat cooperative maritime security as an alternative to hard sea power. Indeed, any suggestion from the United States, or from Chinese proponents, that cooperation would obviate the need for investment in Chinese anti-naval and naval capabilities would likely backfire. By the same token, the United States should not expect East Asian maritime partnership to eliminate the vulnerability problem and should, as already noted, proceed with measures to update its naval capabilities. Indeed, Chinese leaders might be more receptive to a cooperative approach if the United States was seen to be reinvigorating its sea power in the Western Pacific. Moreover, regional maritime cooperation, as envisioned here, would not limit U.S. options in the event of war.

All the same, if multilateral maritime security is pursued, and China elects to join, the risks of confrontation, miscalculation, incidents, and escalation should be more manageable than otherwise. The practicalities of cooperation at sea should make clashes at sea less likely, even if the parties' capabilities are unaffected. As long as the United States does not treat cooperation as an alternative to hard sea power, this is a chance to advance its regional interests, protect its security interests, and add another dimension to the sort of Sino-American partnership it generally wants.

Conclusion

Sea power has long defined the U.S. commitment to East Asia, in war and peace. But it is not the only instrument of U.S. influence. Equally important are U.S. security relationships with old allies and new partners. The United States can build on these relationships to counter

Chinese aggression, should it occur, or, better yet, to persuade China to participate in cooperative maritime security.

China's increased military power and assertiveness are having two strategic effects in the region. As explained in previous chapters, Chinese A2AD capabilities, especially anti-naval targeting and strike systems, are making exposed U.S. forces, e.g., aircraft carriers, vulnerable. The other effect of China's growing military power, thus far, is the clamoring of its neighbors for U.S. re-commitment and steady engagement. These two effects are related in that awareness of the vulnerability of U.S. forces compounds unease in the region about China's advantages. The United States can insist all it wants that it will maintain its strong force presence in the region, but if the survivability of those forces in the event of war is in doubt, U.S. influence will wane as China's power waxes.

The preceding chapter proposed a way for the United States to escape its strategic predicament in East Asia by shifting toward a more distributed, more diverse, more elusive, less observable, and less kinetic sea-based posture. But it also acknowledged that the U.S. Navy would take many years if not decades to transform its concentrated surface fleet. As a consequence, the vulnerability problem will get worse before it gets better. Though this does mean a spike in the probability of war with China, it also means that the region could become unstable, that maritime security could suffer, that regional states could lose confidence in the United States, and that a Chinese sphere of influence could develop.

Even if its technological options could take decades to implement, the United States has political options that it could take without delay. It can organize cooperative regional maritime security. Its intent should not be to isolate China, which would be difficult and could make the Chinese more antagonistic and determined to target U.S. forces. Rather, the United States, with the support of its regional partners, should endeavor to include China in collective maritime security. As the "price of admission," China would have to accept restraints on threats to maritime security, obligations to settle disputes peacefully and consensually, and de facto acceptance of the legitimacy of U.S. sea power in the Western Pacific.

Success would depend heavily on convincing the Chinese that (a) regional maritime cooperation will proceed in any case and (b) their participation in it is honestly sought. Enticing the Chinese to join such an initiative may be a long shot, at least at first. Yet, the benefits of success would be great enough to justify trying despite the odds. The United States and the region would be better off organizing naval cooperation even without China than they otherwise would be. While U.S. diplomats would likely warn of the danger of alienating the Chinese, they are skilled enough to package and present this approach in a way that welcomes China. After all, while the criteria described above are not ideal from the Chinese standpoint—indeed, would be objectionable—they are totally consistent with accepted norms regarding the seas. The United States has repeatedly urged China to become a "responsible stakeholder" in the international system. Inviting China to be a founding and key member of a new East Asian maritime security system would further that American goal.

Recalling the Anglo-German case, it may be that strategic considerations would dissuade the United States from proposing cooperative maritime security or China from accepting it. Like Great Britain before World War I, America today might reject any constraint on the use of its sea dominance. Like Imperial Germany, China might conclude that only the end of its rival's dominance would satisfy its strategic need for world access. Perhaps Mahan's belief that sea powers were destined to compete is as true in the 21st century as it was in the 19th. If so, the United States and China will intensify a costly and potentially dangerous struggle for advantage at the other's expense. Although East Asian maritime partnership would not put limits on capabilities or foreclose options in the event of war, it could build confidence and show that there is room for two sea powers in the Western Pacific.

CHAPTER SIX

Conclusions and Recommendations

"Naval strategy is as necessary in peace as in war."
—A. T. Mahan[1]

The Need for American Initiative

It is worth considering the Sino-American case in the framework used in Chapter Two to assess historical cases. This facilitates both a comparison with those cases and a "net assessment" of the risks and opportunities for American sea power in the Western Pacific. Table 3 thus presents the three historical comparisons shown in Table 1, along with a summary of the current Sino-U.S. case.

What does this reveal? First, China and the United States are as reliant on oceanic trade as the great sea-power rivals of old. Like 19th-century Germany, Japan, and the United States itself, 21st-century China will be impelled to oppose a sea-denial strategy of the established power. Though currently well behind the United States in the capacity to achieve sea power, China has the economic, industrial, and technological potential to mount a strong challenge in the Western Pacific. Developing in phases like that of earlier challengers, Chinese sea power began with coastal defense, is being extended to drive threats beyond striking distance of its territory, and will soon encompass Chinese territorial claims in resource-rich adjacent seas. Chinese sea power takes the form of anti-naval capabilities—power *of* the seas if not *upon* the seas. Whether or not China will become a full-fledged global sea power is unclear and, for now, less important than its intentions in the Western

[1] Alfred T. Mahan, *The Influence of Sea Power upon History, 1660–1783*, p. 89, quoted in Hattendorf, 1991.

Table 3
Comparison of Sino-U.S. Sea-Power Rivalry with Historical Cases

	Great Britain (GB) and the United States (US)	Great Britain and Imperial Germany (IG)	The United States and Imperial Japan (IJ)	The United States and China
Reliance on sea-borne trade	GB: High US: Medium (and growing)	GB: High IG: Medium (and growing)	US: Medium IJ: High	US: High China: High
Bilateral economic interdependence	High	Medium	Low	High
Relative economic and industrial capacity and potential	GB: High US: High (and growing)	GB: High IG: High (and growing)	US: High IJ: Medium	US: High China: High (and growing)
Naval technology, skill, and experience	GB: High US: Medium (and growing)	GB: High IG: Medium (and growing)	US: High IJ: High	US: High China: Medium (and growing)
Conflicting national interests, including contested spheres of influence	Low	Medium	High	Mixed (medium regionally, low globally)
Potential for cooperative maritime security	High	Medium (not pursued)	Low	Medium
Political influence of naval interests	GB: High US: High	GB: High IG: High	US: Medium IJ: High	US: Medium China: Medium
Outcome	Accommodation, cooperation, alliance	Contributed to antagonism and likelihood of war	Primary cause and instruments of war	Competition or cooperation?

Pacific. Even if the Chinese do not choose to build a full-fledged blue-water fleet—which would be vulnerable to U.S. targeting—they will at least follow through on current efforts to hold U.S. sea power at risk in the Western Pacific.

What does this analytic framework suggest about how an established sea power and rising sea power can achieve cooperation instead of competition and confrontation? For one thing, the absence of strong economic interdependence and convergence of other interests, as in the Japanese-U.S. case, is inauspicious. In addition, when the rising power lacks the potential to compete with or successfully confront the established one, the established one has less incentive to accommodate and cooperate with the rising one. Imperial Japan, for all its strengths, did not have the industrial scale or economic model to challenge the United States if the United States chose to oppose it, which it did. In sharp contrast, the British knew they could not prevail against a determined American challenge. Moreover, because British and American interests were increasingly convergent and their economies strongly linked, British leaders determined that accommodating and eventually cooperating with U.S. sea power was better than the alternative. In contrast, the British did not see Germany as too formidable to oppose, yet they did see German strategy in Europe and beyond as threatening to Britain's core interests. So they opted to compete and confront, and they never offered cooperation.

China's scale and industrial-technological potential is such that the United States cannot afford to be cocky about sea-power rivalry in the Western Pacific. Moreover, Chinese and American economic and security interests are in general compatible globally, and this includes the security of oceanic trade. This means there is some potential for maritime security cooperation along the lines suggested here. It is in the interests of the established power to offer this and of the rising power to accept that offer—if rationality and statesmanship prevail.

It could take decades for China to marshal the requisite skills, experience, and doctrine to become an authentic sea power, as it took Germany, Japan, and the United States, all of which were highly developed countries. But the Chinese threat to U.S. sea power is coming much faster. Current technology, which China is readily acquiring and applying, can improve Chinese targeting more than it can improve U.S. survivability.

The United States and China are like Great Britain and the United States in the late 19th century, but also like Great Britain and Germany in the same age. Great Britain's interests in the Western Hemisphere did not warrant rivalry with rising U.S. sea power. Though it ended peacefully and in mutual benefit, the Anglo-American case is not the model for today because the United States cannot allow China an East Asian equivalent of the Monroe Doctrine. Assuming American interests dictate remaining a power in the Western Pacific, as this entire study does, the Anglo-German case is more pertinent because British interests in Europe demanded that Germany's challenge be met—thus the challenge to American and Chinese statesmanship.

As in the Anglo-German case, Chinese and American interests are more compatible globally than regionally—that is, near China. Likewise, China and the United States have a high degree of economic interdependence and a common interest in secure trade, as did Great Britain and Germany. Yet these factors did not prevent sea-power rivalry between Great Britain and Germany—and so far are not preventing sea-power rivalry between China and the United States.

Naval politics in the Sino-American case are not what they were in the Anglo-German case, when political leaders in both capitals were sold not just on the need for sea power but on the imperative of competition. This led to a failure to pursue, or even to consider, a cooperative approach to maritime security. Today's U.S. and Chinese navies lack the political clout that the British and German navies had at the height of their rivalry. Moreover, the U.S. Navy has expressed an interest in cooperative maritime security in general and with the Chinese Navy in particular.

The voice of the Chinese admirals could be critical in determining the interaction of Chinese and American sea power in the Western Pacific. They are framing the case for Chinese sea power not as a naval requirement but as a national requirement (just as Mahan proposed), and they are gung-ho to establish Chinese sea denial in the region. With challenging U.S. sea power and controlling maritime resources in the region among China's highest national priorities, the Chinese Navy could become very influential, like the Imperial German and Imperial Japanese navies were at a similar juncture. Also like the German and Japanese cases, Chinese civilian control of the military, including the navy, appears to be weaker now than at any time during communist rule.[2]

Even at the political level, the Sino-American case likely will not be resolved as harmoniously as the Anglo-American one was. Again, the United States cannot accept a Chinese sphere of influence as Great Britain accepted an American one. However, China and the United States need not follow the course of Britain and Germany—to arms race, confrontation, and conflict. It depends on whether American statesmen, including those in naval uniforms, react to China in a more creative and less rigid way than British leaders reacted to Germany—by pursuing collective maritime security.

The United States cannot count on Chinese acceptance of an East Asia maritime partnership. Indeed, it seems like a long shot, especially with the PLAN's probable opposition. Yet, if the United States proceeds with such a partnership, it will find itself at the very least with most states of the region organized multilaterally under its leadership to strengthen maritime security. Even without Chinese accession, such an outcome would provide a durable and flexible new political and operating framework for American sea power in the Western Pacific. This approach would capitalize on the most important political advantages the United States has: allies and others in the region that look to it for leadership. It is not clear how long this advantage will last if the United States does not seize the initiative.

Regional maritime partnership would not, however, spare U.S. sea power from China's growing anti-naval capabilities, which will undoubtedly grow regardless of how the United States and its part-

---

[2] Evidence of a loosening of Chinese political control of the military includes weak oversight over cyber-war and ASAT plans, the conduct of operations leading to international incidents, perfunctory civilian direction of the state's Military Commission, and the surprise test-flight of a new Chinese stealth aircraft during a visit to China by the U.S. Secretary of Defense. The underlying reasons include the lack of military service on the part of China's more recent civilian leaders and their willingness, since the mid-1990s, to allow the PLA more autonomy in return for removing itself from the commercial businesses.

ners organize. Therefore, the United States should capitalize on its other important advantage, while it too lasts: technological superiority. The United States clings to its traditional surface posture at its own operational risk and ultimate political risk. The aircraft carrier will remain the core of U.S. naval capabilities globally for decades to come, given its benefits and the absence of advanced anti-naval threats in other regions. But in the Western Pacific, less vulnerable, diverse, elusive, networked strike platforms need to be developed and introduced expeditiously.

The Future of Sea Power

Sea power has come to be synonymous with the theory—and the person—of Alfred Thayer Mahan. However, history will show that it entered a post-Mahan stage at the start of the 21st century, owing to a related pair of developments usually called the information revolution and globalization. For reasons explained in prior chapters, and summarized in Table 4, several—not all—tenets of sea power as conceived by Mahan (and as practiced by the sea powers of his era) are being upset.

If these changes—or at least trends in these directions—are correct, they have significant implications for American and Chinese sea power. It will be difficult for the United States to maintain sea control in the Western Pacific, defined as the ability to use the seas in defiance of the will of others. But neither will the Chinese be able to achieve sea control.

If it is true that technology is making sea denial easier and sea control harder, and also true that economic integration is reinforcing mutual interest in maritime security, it follows that the United States and China—this century's established power and rising power, respectively—should seek a way to cooperate instead of compete at sea.

Like rising powers of the late 19th century—Germany, Japan, and the United States—China may feel its position is too weak to cooperate with the stronger power. The United States does indeed have current advantages: allies and technology. But they may not last. The

Table 4
The Future of Mahan's Ideas

Mahan	The Future
Because of the importance of trade, becoming a sea power is necessary to becoming and remaining a world power.	Still generally true.
Because world politics are inherently competitive, rising sea powers must confront established sea powers.	Cooperative maritime security can offer an alternative to sea-power competition and confrontation.
Sea denial requires sea control.	Sea denial can be achieved without having sea control.
Offense is paramount; defense is important only to enable offense.	Technology will favor anti-naval capabilities.
Sea power is power *upon* the sea.	Power *upon* the sea does not assure sea power.
The essential core of sea power is the offensive strength of the surface fleet.	Sea power will have many components: surface-based missiles, manned and unmanned naval aviation, submarines, land-based aviation, land-based missiles, ASAT, and cyber-war.

time is right for American initiatives to secure the seas for itself and others—including China, if it is willing to join.

One implication of current technological trends is that sea control will become more difficult and sea denial easier in the Western Pacific, for now, and ultimately elsewhere. Another is that sea power can be achieved, and threatened, in a growing number of ways, owing to technological change. Future sea powers are unlikely to favor old-fashioned surface fleets, when submarines, drones, missiles, land-based air-strike forces, and cyber-war capabilities offer more effective and less vulnerable ways of exerting power at sea.

In closing, this book's conclusion is different than its hypothesis. As China challenges American sea power in the Western Pacific—a rising power refusing to defer to an established one—it was worth considering how theory and history illuminated the case at hand. As it turns out, technology has made naval rivalry—fleet for fleet—a thing of the past. Global sensing and pin-point long-range targeting are making the surface of the seas potentially less safe for navies and shipping alike. Fortuitously, globalization increases the incentives for nations, even world powers, to seek security for their ships, their trade, and their economies in partnership instead of as adversaries.

How the United States responds to the growing Chinese threat to its sea power in the Western Pacific could determine whether the dangers of technology or the promise of cooperation will prevail. It could also determine whether the United States can find a modus vivendi in this vital and contested region, clearing the way to the sort of global partnership that would serve U.S. interests.

References

Bitzinger, Richard A., "Recent Developments in Naval and Maritime Modernization in the Asia-Pacific: Implications for Regional Security," in Phillip Saunders, Christopher Yung, Michael Swaine, and Andrew Nien-Dzu Yang, eds., *The Chinese Navy: Expanding Capabilities, Evolving Roles*, Washington, D.C.: National Defense University Press, 2011, pp. 23–40.

Borneman, Walter R., *The Admirals: Nimitz, Halsey, Leahy, and King—the Five-Star Admirals Who Won the War at Sea*, New York: Little, Brown and Company, 2012.

Broz, J. Lawrence, "The U.S. and World Economy in the 19th Century," February 2012. As of December 18, 2012:
http://weber.ucsd.edu/~jlbroz/Courses/Lund/handouts/Lecture4_Politics_World_%20Economy.pdf

Butler, Chris, "The Spread of Industrialization Beyond Britain (c. 1850–1900)," 2007. As of December 4, 2012:
http://www.flowofhistory.com/units/eme/17/FC116

Center for Strategic and International Studies, *U.S. Force Posture in the Asia Pacific Region: An Independent Assessment*, Washington, D.C., July 2012.

Chambers, John Whiteclay II, ed., *The Oxford Companion to American Military History*, New York: Oxford University Press, 1999.

Crammond, Edgar, "The Economic Relations of the British and German Empires," *Journal of the Royal Statistical Society*, Vol. 77, No. 8, July 1914.

Dobbins, James, David C. Gompert, David A. Shlapak, and Andrew Scobell, *Conflict with China: Prospects, Consequences, and Strategies for Deterrence*, Santa Monica, Calif.: RAND Corporation, OP-344, 2011. As of November 29, 2012:
http://www.rand.org/pubs/occasional_papers/OP344.html

Easton, Ian, "The Assassin Under the Radar: China's DH-10 Cruise Missile Program," Project 2049 Institute, Futuregram 09-005, 2009.

The Economist, "Being Eaten by the Dragon; Chinese Takeovers," November 13, 2010.

———, "Smoke Without Fire?" June 2–8, 2012.

Erickson, Andrew S., and Michael S. Chase, "Information and the Chinese People's Liberation Army Navy," in Phillip Saunders, Christopher Yung, Michael Swaine, and Andrew Nien-Dzu Yang, eds., *The Chinese Navy: Expanding Capabilities, Evolving Roles*, Washington, D.C.: National Defense University Press, 2011, pp. 247–286.

Fravel, M. Taylor, "Revisiting Deng's Foreign Policy," taylorfravel.com, January 17, 2012. As of December 5, 2012:
http://taylorfravel.com/2012/01/revising-dengs-foreign-policy/

Glazer, Bonnie, and Brittany Billingsley, "U.S. Pivot to Asia Leaves China Off Balance," *Comparative Connections: A Triannual E-Journal on East Asian Bilateral Relations*, January 2012.

Gompert, David C., *Right Makes Might: Freedom and Power in the Information Age*, Washington, D.C.: National Defense University Press, 1998.

Gompert, David C., Paul K. Davis, Stuart E. Johnson, and Duncan Long, *Analysis of Strategy and Strategies of Analysis*, Santa Monica, Calif.: RAND Corporation, MG-718-JS, 2008. As of November 29, 2012:
http://www.rand.org/pubs/monographs/MG718.html

Gompert, David C., and Phillip Saunders, *The Paradox of Power: Sino-American Strategic Restraint in an Age of Vulnerability*, Washington, D.C.: National Defense University Press, 2011.

Hartnett, Daniel M., and Frederic Vellucci, "Toward a Maritime Security Strategy: An Analysis of Chinese Views Since the Early 1990s," in Phillip Saunders, Christopher Yung, Michael Swaine, and Andrew Nien-Dzu Yang, eds., *The Chinese Navy: Expanding Capabilities, Evolving Roles*, Washington, D.C.: National Defense University Press, 2011, pp. 81–108.

Hattendorf, John B., ed., *Mahan on Naval Strategy: Selections from the Writings of Rear Admiral Alfred Thayer Mahan*, Annapolis, Md.: Naval Institute Press, 1991.

International Monetary Fund World Economic Outlook Databases, web page, June 2011. As of January 7, 2013:
http://www.imf.org/external/ns/cs.aspx?id=28

Irving, John, *The Smoke Screen of Jutland*, New York: David McKay Company, 1966.

Johnson, Stuart E., and Arthur K. Cebrowski, *Alternative Fleet Architecture Design*, Defense and Technology Paper 319, Fort McNair, Washington, D.C.: National Defense University Press, 2005.

Krepinevich, Andrew F., *Why AirSea Battle?* Washington, D.C.: Center for Strategic and Budgetary Assessments, 2010.

Livezey, William E., *Mahan on Sea Power*, Norman, Okla.: University of Oklahoma Press, 1947.

Mackinder, John Halford, *Democratic Ideals and Reality: A Study in the Politics of Reconstruction*, London: Constable and Company, 1919.

Mahan, Alfred T., *The Interest of America in Sea Power, Present and Future*, London: Sampson Low, Marston, and Company, 1897.

———, *Lessons of the War with Spain and Other Articles*, Boston: Little, Brown and Company, 1899.

———, *Sea Power in Its Relation to the War of 1812*, London: Sampson Low, Marston, and Company, 1905.

———, *Some Neglected Aspects of War*, Boston: Little, Brown and Company, 1907.

———, *The Interest of America in International Conditions*, London: Sampson Low, Marston, and Company, 1910.

———, *The Problem of Asia and Its Effect upon International Policies*, Boston: Little, Brown and Company, 1910.

———, "The Importance of Command of the Sea: For an Adequate Navy, and More," *Scientific American*, Vol. 105, No. 24, December 1911.

———, *Naval Strategy: Compared and Contrasted with the Principles and Practice of Military Operations on Land*, London: Sampson Low, Marston, and Company, 1911.

———, *The Influence of Sea Power upon History, 1660–1783*, New York: Sagamore Press, (1890) 1957.

Massie, Robert K., *Dreadnought: Britain, Germany, and the Coming of the Great War*, New York: Ballantine Books, 1991.

McDevitt, Michael, "The PLA Navy's Antiaccess Role in a Taiwan Contingency," in Phillip Saunders, Christopher Yung, Michael Swaine, and Andrew Nien-Dzu Yang, eds., *The Chinese Navy: Expanding Capabilities, Evolving Roles*, Washington, D.C.: National Defense University Press, 2011, pp. 191–214.

Miles, Donna, "U.S., China to Consider Sharing Resources During Joint Missions," Armed Forces Press Service, October 12, 2012. As of December 5, 2012:
http://www.defense.gov/news/newsarticle.aspx?id=118202

Millet, Allan, Peter Maslowksi, and William Feis, *For the Common Defense: A Military History of the United States from 1607 to 2012*, New York: Free Press, 2012.

Mullen, Mike, "A Global Network of Nations for a Free and Secure Maritime Commons," speech at Naval War College, Newport, R.I., September 2005.

Nathan, Andrew, and Andrew Scobell, "How China Sees America," *Foreign Affairs*, September/October 2012.

Naval History and Heritage Command, website, no date. As of December 4, 2012: http://www.history.navy.mil/

———, "U.S. Navy Active Ship Force Levels, 1886–Present," 2011. As of December 4, 2012:
http://www.history.navy.mil/branches/org9-4.htm

O'Rourke, Ronald, "PLAN Force Structure: Submarines, Ships, and Aircraft," in Phillip Saunders, Christopher Yung, Michael Swaine, and Andrew Nien-Dzu Yang, eds., *The Chinese Navy: Expanding Capabilities, Evolving Roles*, Washington, D.C.: National Defense University Press, 2011, pp. 141–174.

———, *China Naval Modernization: Implications for U.S. Navy Capabilities—Background and Issues for Congress*, Washington, D.C.: Congressional Research Service, RL33153, October 17, 2012.

Overholt, William H., *Asia, America, and the Transformation of Geopolitics*, Cambridge University Press, New York, 2008.

People's Republic of China, *China's National Defense in 2004*, white paper, 2004. As of December 7, 2012:
http://www.china.org.cn/english/2004/Dec/116032.htm

———, *China's National Defense in 2010*, white paper, 2010. As of December 7, 2012:
http://www.china.org.cn/government/whitepaper/node_7114675.htm

Potter, E. B., and Chester W. Nimitz, eds., *Sea Power: A Naval History*, Upper Saddle River, N.J.: Prentice-Hall, 1960.

Pulleston, W. D., *Mahan: The Life and Work of Alfred Thayer Mahan, USN*, New Haven, Conn.: Yale University Press, 1939.

Rahman, Chris, *The Global Maritime Partnership Initiative: Implications for the Royal Australian Navy*, Australian Department of Defence, 2008.

Ravitch, Samantha, *Marketization and Democracy: East Asian Experiences*, New York: Cambridge University Press, 1999.

Richardson, Doug, "China Plans 4,000 Km–Range Conventional Ballistic Missile," *Jane's Missiles and Rockets*, March 1, 2011.

Saunders, Phillip, Christopher Yung, Michael Swaine, and Andrew Nien-Dzu Yang, eds., *The Chinese Navy: Expanding Capabilities, Evolving Roles*, Washington, D.C.: National Defense University Press, 2011.

Schwartz, Norton A. (Gen., USAF), and Jonathan W. Greenert (Adm., USN), "Air-Sea Battle: Promoting Stability in an Era of Uncertainty," *The American Interest*, February 20, 2012.

Stokes, Mark A., Prepared Statement for U.S.-China Economic and Security Review Commission hearing on the Implications of China's Military and Civil Space Programs, May 11, 2011.

Swaine, Michael D., "Chinese Leadership and Elite Responses to the U.S. Pacific Pivot," *China Leadership Monitor*, No. 38, Summer 2012. As of December 18, 2012:
http://carnegieendowment.org/2012/07/17/chinese-leadership-and-elite-responses-to-u.s.-pacific-pivot/cuk3

Swartz, Peter M., "Rising Powers and Naval Powers," in Phillip Saunders, Christopher Yung, Michael Swaine, and Andrew Nien-Dzu Yang, eds., *The Chinese Navy: Expanding Capabilities, Evolving Roles*, Washington, D.C.: National Defense University Press, 2011, pp. 1–22.

Taylor, Charles C., *The Life of Admiral Mahan*, New York: Doran Co., 1920.

Thomas, Evan, *The War Lovers: Roosevelt, Lodge, Hearst, and the Rush to Empire, 1898*, New York: Little, Brown and Company, 2010.

"Tokyo Seeks to Expand Defense Against China," *Wall Street Journal*, July 12, 2012, p. 14.

The United States Strategic Bombing Survey, *The Effects of Strategic Bombing on Japan's War Economy*, December 1946.

U.S. Census Bureau, *2012 Statistical Abstract*, Washington, D.C., 2012.

U.S. Department of Defense, *Military and Security Developments Involving the People's Republic of China*, Annual Report to Congress, 2010.

Vernon, Raymond, *Sovereignty at Bay: The Multinational Spread of U.S. Enterprises*, New York: Basic Books, 1971.

The White House, *Sustaining U.S. Global Leadership: Priorities for 21st Century Defense*, January 2012.